Fighting
Spam
FOR
DUMMIES®

by John R. Levine,
Margaret Levine Young,
Ray Everett-Church

WILEY

Wiley Publishing, Inc.

Fighting Spam For Dummies®

Published by
Wiley Publishing, Inc.
111 River Street
Hoboken, NJ 07030-5774

WILEY

About the Authors

John R. Levine was a member of a computer club in high school — before high school students, or even high schools, had computers — where he met Theodor H. Nelson, the author of *Computer Lib/Dream Machines* and the inventor of hypertext, who reminded us that computers should not be taken seriously and that everyone can and should understand and use computers.

John wrote his first program in 1967 on an IBM 1130 (a computer somewhat less powerful than your typical modern digital wristwatch, only more difficult to use). He became an official system administrator of a networked computer at Yale in 1975. He began working part-time, for a computer company, of course, in 1977 and has been in and out of the computer and network biz ever since. Since he has been on the Internet for a long time, he started getting spammed early and often, leading to his joining the board of the Coalition Against Unsolicited Commercial E-mail (CAUCE) and starting the Network Abuse Clearinghouse (www.abuse.net).

Although John used to spend most of his time writing software, now he mostly writes books (including *The Internet For Dummies* and *Internet Secrets,* both published by Wiley Publishing, Inc.) because it's more fun and he can do so at home in the tiny village of Trumansburg, New York, where he is the sewer commissioner (Guided tours! Free samples!) and can play with his small daughter when he's supposed to be writing. John also does a fair amount of public speaking. (See www.iecc.com/john1 to see where he'll be.) He holds a B.A. and a Ph.D. in computer science from Yale University, but please don't hold that against him.

Margaret Levine Young was a member of the same high-school computer club as John (probably because she was his little sister at the time). She stayed in the field throughout college against her better judgment and despite John's presence as a graduate student in the computer science department. Margy graduated from Yale and went on to become one of the first PC managers in the early 1980s at Columbia Pictures, where she rode the elevator with big stars whose names she wouldn't dream of dropping here.

Since then, Margy has coauthored more than 25 books about the Internet, Unix, Microsoft Access, online communities, WordPerfect, and (stab from the past) PC-File and Javelin, including *The Internet For Dummies* and *Access 2003 All-in-One Desk Reference For Dummies* (published by Wiley Publishing, Inc.) and *Windows XP Home Edition: The Complete Reference* and *Internet: The Complete Reference* (published by Osborne/ McGraw-Hill). She met her future husband, Jordan, in the R.E.S.I.S.T.O.R.S. (that computer club we mentioned). Her other passions are her children, Unitarian Universalism (www.uua.org), and cooking. She lives in Vermont (see www.gurus.com/margy).

Ray Everett-Church published his first article about computers — and about the mischief one could cause with them — in a community newspaper in Nashville, Tennessee, back in 1983. Nobody has been able to shut him up since.

In 1999, he became the world's first corporate chief privacy officer, and has spent much of his career since then teaching Fortune 500 firms how to respect consumer privacy and avoid being labeled as spammers.

He received degrees from George Mason University and the George Washington University Law School. During law school, he supported himself by working as an antispam consultant to an upstart online service named America Online. He trains dozens of privacy professionals each year in executive seminars and lectures, and has testified before Congress and the U.S. Federal Trade Commission on the issues of junk e-mail and online marketing.

Ray now works as chief privacy officer for the privacy and antispam technology company ePrivacy Group (www.eprivacygroup.com), where he heads its consulting division. He lives a stone's throw from Silicon Valley, in always lovely northern California, with his very patient partner, Justin, and two rather strange-looking cats. You can learn more about Ray at www.everett.org.

Dedication

John dedicates his part of the book to Tonia and Sarah, again and forever. Margy dedicates her part to Jordan, Meg, and Zac, as always. Ray dedicates his part to his Mom and Dad, and to Justin.

Authors' Acknowledgments

All three authors would like to thank the folks at Wiley Publishing, Inc., for making this book happen, including Steve Hayes, Rebecca Whitney (the world's best editor), and the rest of the gang listed on the Publisher's Acknowledgments page.

Ray gives thanks to Vince Schiavone, Stephen Cobb, David Brussin, Lucinda Duncalfe Holt, Michael Miora, and the outstanding team at ePrivacy Group for their friendship and professional prowess in privacy, security, and spam fighting; David Lawrence and Lili von Schtupp, from "The David Lawrence Show" and "Online Tonight," for their friendship and occasional airtime; and to the members of the Cabal (TINC) — you know who you are, which of course means that you're now going to have to be killed. Sorry we brought it up.

Margy thanks the gang at AnswerSquad.com, for answering various technical questions, and to her friends and family for putting up with the process of writing and editing yet another book.

Publisher's Acknowledgments

We're proud of this book; please send us your comments through our online registration form located at www.dummies.com/register/.

Some of the people who helped bring this book to market include the following:

Acquisitions, Editorial, and Media Development

Project Editor: Rebecca Whitney

Acquisitions Editor: Steve Hayes

Technical Editor: James F. Kelly

Editorial Manager: Carol Sheehan

Media Development Supervisor: Richard Graves

Editorial Assistant: Amanda M. Foxworth

Cartoons: Rich Tennant (www.the5thwave.com)

Production

Project Coordinator: Erin Smith

Layout and Graphics: Lauren Goddard, LeAndra Hosier, Stephanie D. Jumper, Michael Kruzil, Lynsey Osborn, Jacque Schneider

Proofreaders: Laura Albert, TECHBOOKS Production Services

Indexer: TECHBOOKS Production Services

Publishing and Editorial for Technology Dummies

　　Richard Swadley, Vice President and Executive Group Publisher

　　Andy Cummings, Vice President and Publisher

　　Mary C. Corder, Editorial Director

Publishing for Consumer Dummies

　　Diane Graves Steele, Vice President and Publisher

　　Joyce Pepple, Acquisitions Director

Composition Services

　　Gerry Fahey, Vice President of Production Services

　　Debbie Stailey, Director of Composition Services

Contents at a Glance

Table of Contents

Introduction

• •

*S*pam — unsolicited bulk and commercial e-mail — may be killing e-mail. Spam is causing people to cancel their Internet accounts (or at least stop reading their e-mail) because e-mail has become an unpleasant waste of time. E-mail has also become unreliable because spam filters sometimes accidentally throw away good messages with the spam. Spam wastes thousands of hours of your time, as you skim Subject lines and press the Delete key, trying to guess which messages aren't even worth opening.

Luckily, you can do something about spam, on both the small scale and the grand scale. On the small scale, you can use spam filters to junk most of the spam that's addressed to you, and you can report spam to network managers. On the grand scale, you can lobby for effective antispam laws to make it possible to sue the rip-off artists who fill your inboxes that *you* pay for with *their* advertising.

You have probably figured out that we have some strong feelings about spam! If you have bought or borrowed this book, you probably have strong feelings too.

This book talks about how you can get rid of most or all of the spam in your mailbox. We also cover where spam comes from, how it came about, whom to report it to, and whether antispam laws would be effective. We can assure you that after reading this book, you will know how to have an almost spam-free Internet experience — how's that for good news?

What's in This Book

This book is divided into four parts so that you can find what you want quickly:

- ✔ Part I, "The World of Spam," describes what spam is, how it works, how spammers get your address, how antispam laws may and should work, and how to complain about spam you receive.

- ✔ Part II, "Filtering Spam Out of Your Inbox," tells you how to create folders and filters in your e-mail program to move spam from your inbox either into another folder or directly into the trash. We describe Outlook Express, Outlook, Netscape Mail, Mozilla Mail, Eudora, AOL, MSN, Hotmail, and Yahoo! Mail. The latest versions of some of these programs already contain powerful spam-filtering features, and we explain how to use them.

- ✔ Part III, "Spam-Filtering Programs and Services," looks at spam-filtering programs you can install on your computer and spam-filtering services that can filter spam from your e-mail even before it arrives on your computer. For network administrators, we describe how to run e-mail servers that include spam filters.

- ✔ Part IV, "The Part of Tens," lists ten spam scams that you should *never* fall for and ten Internet annoyances — like browser pop-ups and missing Web pages — and their solutions.

Conventions and Icons in This Book

When you need to give a command in a Windows, Mac, or other windowing system, we show the command like this: File⇨Open. Choose File from the menu bar and then click Open on the menu that appears. When we tell you to press Ctrl+N, hold down the Ctrl (Control) key, press N, and release the Ctrl key.

We use some icons in the left margin to tell you when something exciting is happening:

Indicates that we're explaining a nifty shortcut or time-saver.

Lets you know that some particularly nerdy, technoid information is coming up so that you can skip it if you want. (On the other hand, we think that it's interesting, and you may too.)

Yikes! We found out the hard way! Don't let this happen to you!

Points to a gentle reminder about an important point.

Write to Us — That's Not Spam!

We love to hear from our readers. Write to us at spamfighting@gurus.com to let us know whether this book reduced the amount of spam you see. You get a message back from our friendly mailbot immediately, and we human readers read the mail too and answer as much as we can.

You can also visit our Internet Gurus Web site, at net.gurus.com, or the *Internet Privacy For Dummies* Web site (which has lots of spam information), at www.internetprivacyfordummies.com. For information about other *For Dummies* books, visit www.dummies.com.

Part I
The World of Spam

"Can't I just give you riches or something?"

In this part . . .

Ten years ago, spam hardly existed, and now it wastes the time of millions of people every day — including you. We recommend a 3-pronged approach to fighting spam: Complain to spammers' ISPs to get them thrown off the Internet, lobby for effective antispam laws, and prevent spam from getting into your mailbox. This part of the book gets you up to speed on where spam comes from, how spammers operate, and what you can do about it — the first two prongs of the antispam triad.

Chapter 1

How Spam Works — and Drives You Crazy!

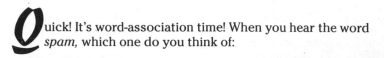

*Q*uick! It's word-association time! When you hear the word *spam,* which one do you think of:

    a. A salty, pink lunch meat that comes in a blue can?

    b. A goofy British comedy troupe's skit with singing Viking warriors?

    c. Annoying junk mail and other advertisements you never asked for that are sent to you via the Internet?

    d. All of the above.

The best answer is

    d. All of the above.

As most people know, *SPAM* (with all capital letters) is a salty, pink lunch meat that is made by Hormel and comes in a blue can.

Hormel, the makers of SPAM (the lunch meat), say that if you want to call junk e-mail by the same name, they don't object. You just can't use all capital letters, like they appear on the can. *SPAM* is lunch meat, and *spam* is junk e-mail. Got it? We're talking about *spam* written with lowercase letters (at the request of Hormel) so that people don't confuse the spam we all hate for the SPAM that some people find tasty.

Spam, Spam, Spam, Spam, Spam, Spam, Spam, Spam

Avid fans of the British comedy team Monty Python may remember the skit where a husband and wife enter a restaurant in a seaside resort town only to find that every dish on the menu features SPAM. Unfortunately, the wife is not at all fond of SPAM and searches in vain for dishes that don't have any of the noxious substance. With SPAM appearing everywhere she turns, her frustration grows.

We're not sure why, but the skit also features a large band of Viking warriors lunching at the dinette who, every time the wife says the meat's name aloud, regularly break into a deafening song about "SPAM, SPAM, SPAM, Lovely SPAM! Wonderful SPAM!" — adding to her confusion and anger. (For true fans of Monty Python, however, singing Vikings at a seaside dinette are par for the course.)

Everyone who uses the Internet has encountered loads and loads of junk advertisements that appear when you least expect them and usually where they're least wanted — namely, in your e-mail inbox and on the message boards and newsgroups you frequent.

Legend has it that someone casting his eye over a menu of newsgroup discussion topics kept seeing the same ads posted in nearly every conversation thread. The continual appearance of these ads in every discussion group reminded this person of Monty Python's seaside café with SPAM appearing in every menu item and conversation being drowned out by the ceaseless monotony of Viking-like advertisers.

In the Monty Python sketch, the distraught SPAM-hating wife finally snaps and screams "I don't like SPAM!!!" If you're like us, you have spent enough time sorting through the junk e-mail in your inbox that you too have found yourself screaming about spam.

Why Spam Works

Anyone who has ever sent an e-mail message knows that it's a quick, simple, and cheap process. After you have a computer and an Internet connection, your investment is finished. To send an e-mail, you don't have to worry about buying envelopes or stamps. You just have to have an e-mail address for somebody, and something to say.

This same economic reality is what spammers depend on. Sending e-mail in bulk costs the sender a tiny fraction of the cost of sending postal mail or making telemarketing phone calls. One person can generate huge volumes of mail with just a few clicks of a mouse, blanketing millions of inboxes in a matter of minutes or hours.

The economics of spam

The economics of e-mail turn all the traditional notions of advertising on their heads. No other advertising medium costs the recipient more than it costs the sender of the ad.

With television, print ads in newspapers, or advertisements via the U.S. Postal Service, the sender has to spend a bundle on printing or other preparation of the ad, delivery, and so forth. The high cost naturally forces advertisers to be a bit picky about how much advertising they send out, and to whom they send it, because each additional ad bears an incremental cost.

In the world of junk e-mail marketing, it costs no more to send the first e-mail than it does to send the ten millionth e-mail. No economic restriction keeps marketers from blasting their advertisements as widely and indiscriminately as possible. They don't even have an incentive to remove duplicate addresses from mailing lists. Why not? When advertisers pay nothing more for each additional message, any time spent on editing a mailing list is time wasted.

Why spam is a bigger problem than you think

We all get postal junk mail. That's an accepted fact of life, at least in the United States. You may wonder why spam is any different.

Spam is different from the junk mail that is mailed to your house or the telemarketing calls that interrupt your dinner, for one simple reason: The people who send you that junk mail and make those phone calls have to pay for the cost of doing so, and the price can be steep. Junk mail has to be written, designed, printed, and collated, and postage must be paid. Telemarketers must rent office space, hire staff members, install phones, and pay long-distance phone charges. We don't say this to defend them, but rather to draw a distinction between the costs that traditional marketers incur and the costs that a spammer *doesn't* incur.

When a spammer sends an ad for herbal Viagra or an XXX-rated Web site or canine harmonica lessons to millions of people over the Internet, she pays almost nothing because, as we all know, e-mail is virtually free to the party who is sending it. But someone has to bear the cost of distributing those millions of e-mails to recipients all over the globe — and therein lies the difference between online unsolicited advertising and offline unsolicited advertising.

There's no such thing as a free lunch, particularly on the Internet

If you're like most people, you pay an Internet service provider (ISP) to get access to the Internet. (Even if your company or school pays for your access, someone is paying for it.) E-mail is one of the services your ISP provides as part of its service to you. For most people, the costs of your e-mail service are simply bundled into your service package. In reality, these costs can form a significant part of your monthly bill (as much as $3 or $4 of a standard $19.95 charge).

It wasn't long ago that ISPs charged per message for Internet e-mail. In the early days (well, 1991, which was pretty early for lots of Internet users), the service provider Prodigy used to charge 25 cents per message!

Even now, users of "free" e-mail services, like Hotmail and Yahoo! Mail, "pay" by being subjected to advertisements all over their mailboxes, and the advertisers pay to run the servers at those sites. What seems to be free is really just costs factored into your service, and the costs related to e-mail don't stop there.

Suppose that you have a friend in Timbuktu whom you love to hear from by e-mail. The data that makes up the e-mail from your friend leaves her computer and begins a wondrous journey though any number of computers and networks on its way to you. Presumably, your friend owns her computer, so the resources used to create the message are largely hers. After that e-mail leaves her computer, though, the entire rest of its journey is spent bouncing around servers and careening down transmission lines that belong to anybody *other than* her — unless, of course, she happens to personally own her own international fiber-optic network!

Considering that most of us don't have a spare data network lying around, when that e-mail is sent, you and your friend are both depending on every service provider and communications network between you and Timbuktu to let that e-mail pass through their networks. In this way, virtually every e-mail is, to one extent or another, sent "postage due," with the postage being paid by everybody along the way.

Spam is a bad deal for everybody (except the spammer)

If you think about it, sending bulk e-mail to millions of people is just as cheap for a spammer as it is for a faraway friend in Timbuktu, especially when it's compared to the cost of sending junk ads by postal mail or telemarketing. After all, a spammer has no printing costs, no stamps to buy, no phones to install, no telemarketers to hire, and no long-distance calls to pay for. Instead, a spammer sends hundreds or thousands of messages per hour for just a fraction of a penny per spam.

Just because a spammer doesn't pay much for sending his spam, though, doesn't mean that someone isn't paying — and you would never guess who's at the head of the list: you.

Just like a friend you may have in Timbuktu, when a spammer decides to send the latest get-rich-quick scheme to 25 million of his closest friends, he can get an account at a local ISP and begin sending mail. After those 25 million messages leave his computer, though, the vast majority of the "postage" for delivering his mail is paid for by the 25 million recipients, their ISPs, and all the other networks, servers, and ISPs in between.

The crushing volumes of spam cost Internet service providers (ISPs) huge amounts of money for all the servers and Internet connection capacity needed to receive, process, store, and deliver unwanted e-mail. Several major ISPs estimated that by the end of 2003, spam would comprise upward of 80 percent of their entire e-mail volume. Imagine if you had to have an 80 percent larger house because your in-laws kept coming to stay. That's a lot of money, not to mention the pain and suffering!

How big of a problem is spam? A study commissioned by the European parliament in 2001 discovered that spam costs about $9.4 billion each year — a huge bill that is being footed by everyone except the spammers themselves. And much more spam is flowing this year than in 2001.

Who Hath Spammed Thee? (The Spammer Food Chain)

To understand the problem of spam, it helps to know who is doing it and what they're advertising. Surveying the Internet, you can quickly see that almost no reputable marketers use spam to advertise goods and services. That doesn't mean that reputable companies don't sometimes send out e-mail that the recipients don't want or didn't expect. But few legitimate companies engage in the kinds of complex spamming campaigns that are responsible for most of what is filling your inbox.

To the contrary, the most commonly mailed spams advertise pyramid schemes, get-rich-quick and make-money-fast scams, phone-sex lines, pornographic Web sites, and quack medical products. Most ironically, vast quantities of spam advertise spamming software, spamming services, and lists of millions of e-mail addresses you can buy so that you too can become a spammer. We have even seen spam advertising antispam filters!

When we talk about *spammers*, we're really talking about at least three categories of people who may be responsible for putting a particular piece of spam in your inbox:

- ✓ Advertisers
- ✓ Spam service providers
- ✓ Spam support services

The first category is the advertiser. You can't have spam without somebody who wants to advertise something. They may be sophisticated technical experts who do their own spamming, or they may be computer illiterates who saw an advertisement and decided to hire a third party to send spam for them. Whoever they may be, they are generally the people responsible for whatever message is contained in the body of the spam, and generally the one to whom you make out the check when it's time to buy the miracle hair-growth and body-part enlargement product.

Spam service providers are people who have built up the hardware, software, and expertise needed to pump out a bazillion spam e-mails. According to many antispam experts, the great majority of the spam you receive comes from a relative handful of professional spam service providers. They advertise their services to the latest sucker — er, "distributor" — of the latest get-rich-quick scheme and charge them a few hundred bucks to send a few million spams. Even though the distributor may never make a penny from the spamming campaign, the spam service provider has made his money, and that's all he cares about.

Spam support services can include ISPs and Web site hosting services that take any customer, no matter what kind of criminal or fraudulent activity they're engaged in. These ISPs are often in areas of the world where the laws may be either different or nonexistent. China, Russia, Brazil, Argentina, and South Korea are among the leading countries where spam service providers have found ISPs willing to provide support services, just as long as the checks keep clearing.

The first spammers

Back in 1994, the U.S. government decided to hold a lottery to give away some permanent resident visas to immigrants seeking to stay in the United States indefinitely. The lottery program gave away several thousand permanent residency visas, still called *green cards* (even though they haven't been green for many decades), to anyone who sent a postcard to a particular address before the deadline date.

Several months before the deadline, on the evening of April 12, 1994, Laurence Canter and Martha Siegel, a husband-and-wife lawyer team, decided to join the lottery frenzy by pitching their own overpriced "lottery services" to immigrant communities. But these two were not your run-of-the-mill hucksters. They were innovators with a penchant for technology. Canter and Siegel chose Usenet newsgroups, and later e-mail, as their advertising vehicles. Neither medium would ever be the same.

Within hours, the Internet service provider used by Canter and Siegel had shut off their access. But the genie was out of the bottle. The era of spam had begun. Within weeks, Canter and Siegel had branched out from newsgroups to e-mail, and in a matter of a few months they had penned the book *How to Make a Fortune on the Information Superhighway,* which detailed their spamming strategies.

Your humble co-author, Ray, had the unfortunate experience of being on the receiving end of many complaints when Canter and Siegel first burst onto the spamming scene in 1994, so the spamming duo holds a special spot in Ray's heart. At the time, he was working for the American Immigration Lawyers Association and was responsible for fielding complaints from angry spam victims who wanted to see the pair disbarred. Not surprisingly, they had already been disbarred once in the state of Florida, and would eventually lose their law licenses from other states as a result of their dishonest spam campaigns.

You can still pick up a (used) copy of their book on Amazon.com, but it's more of a historical footnote than a useful how-to guide. Indeed, you can draw a much more informative lesson from looking at where these morally bankrupt business ideas landed the pair: disbarred, dead at an early age (in the case of Ms. Siegel), and writing software manuals (in the case of Mr. Canter).

Canter and Siegel were trailblazers in another sense too: Their past legal problems seem to be a harbinger of success in the spamming business. Many of the most notorious spammers now have criminal records and convictions for fraud and drug offenses and have even spent time in jail.

The Father of the Internet speaks out about spam

"Spamming is the scourge of electronic-mail and newsgroups on the Internet. It can seriously interfere with the operation of public services, to say nothing of the effect it may have on any individual's e-mail mail system. Spammers are, in effect, taking resources away from users and service suppliers without compensation and without authorization."

— Vint Cerf, acknowledged "Father of the Internet"

Why "Just Hit the Delete Key!" Is No Answer

Although spammers love to say "Just hit the Delete key," it totally misses the point. By the time the spam hits the fan (well, when it hits all our mailboxes), so many costs have been incurred by so many people other than the spammer that it is either naïve or an utter act of denial to pretend that those costs can be undone with the pressing of one key.

Spam is about the numbers, so let's look at some numbers that show why hitting the Delete key isn't really a workable solution. The U.S. Small Business Administration estimates that the United States has approximately 25 million businesses. If only 1 percent of those 25 million decides to send you just one single unsolicited e-mail per year, you average 685 spams *per day* in your inbox. If it takes an average of 10 seconds per message to open a message, determine that it is spam, and hit Delete, you spend two hours per day disposing of e-mail you never asked to receive.

More Ways You Pay for Spam

For your Internet service provider (ISP), the costs associated with processing incoming e-mail are the same, whether or not it's e-mail that its customers want. The more e-mail your ISP processes, the higher those costs. As spam volumes increase, it begins to clog Internet bandwidth and begins to fill up the storage disks on your ISP's servers. Whenever you're trying to surf the Web, therefore, you're competing with spam for the use of your ISP's Internet connection, slowing you down when you're surfing.

With overworked servers receiving and storing spam for hundreds of thousands of users, your access to your own e-mail can also slow down. E-mail servers are powerful machines, capable of doing thousands of tasks per second, but even those big machines can get bogged down. And when you're eager to read your e-mail, the last thing you want is to have to compete with some spammer for access to your ISP's mail servers.

Every once in a while, an ISP gets so overloaded with spam that its servers crash. This situation causes everybody who was depending on that server to be inconvenienced. It may also be more than an inconvenience if, for example, your company's e-commerce Web site was on that same server or a bunch of customers' orders were in the e-mails that got scrambled when the server gave up the ghost. Calculating the cost in terms of lost business opportunities when customers can't reach you or think that you're ignoring them is almost impossible, but those are more costs you bear, thanks to spammers.

Eventually, if the service quality gets too bad, to keep subscribers from jumping to a competitor, an ISP begins buying more Internet bandwidth and more servers. Of course, it needs to be hiring more staff members to install that equipment and to keep everything running. At some point, those costs get passed back to you — perhaps in the form of rate hikes or longer hold times when you call your ISP for customer service. While he was working on this book, co-author John, who provides mail service for a few dozen friends and web-hosting users on his tiny network, had to spend about $1,000 upgrading the mail server, just to deal with the increase in spam.

The number of unsolicited messages sent out each day is truly remarkable. The spam-filtering company Brightmail claims that its research has shown more than 25 million unsolicited messages being sent per day in 1998. By 2002, AOL and Hotmail both claimed that they were blocking nearly a billion pieces of spam each day, and still more was slipping through. According to a September 2003 survey by *InformationWeek*, spam volumes were growing at 37 percent per month, for an annual growth rate of more than 400 percent!

Numerous court cases are under way between spammers and innocent victims who have been subjected to these types of floods. Unfortunately, although major corporations can afford to fight these cutting-edge cyberlaw battles, small mom-and-pop ISPs and their customers are left to suffer the floods.

Here's another cost you may not have thought of: your time. Because of the volume of spam zipping around the Internet, downloading your e-mail takes longer. Although you may call a local number to connect with the Internet, lots of other people pay by the minute for the time they spend online. Because of spam, it takes them longer to get their e-mail, and spam costs them money in connection charges every month.

Calling Erin Brockovich!

If you saw the movie *Erin Brockovich* (which was based on a true story), you know that the sassy heroine does battle with a polluting power company that has dumped nasty gunk into the groundwater, which is causing the citizens in a nearby town to become quite sick. Oddly enough, noxious floods of spam have a similar effect on the health of the Internet and all the netizens who use it.

The reason that companies dump toxic waste into lakes and rivers is that they have done the math. It may cost them many millions of dollars per year to properly dispose of the waste from one plant. Or, they can just dump it into the river for free.

Economists call the toxic waste an *externality*, which is their word for something that gets generated as a by-product of someone's moneymaking activity, the cost of which gets "paid for" by all the citizens who then have a greater risk of disease.

If the pollution levels stay relatively low, some people may never notice that they're slowly being poisoned and they may eventually die of something else. Occasionally, though, somebody does get sick, and for them, the cost of that pollution suddenly becomes great. As in the movie, companies gamble that the amount they may have to pay for an occasional illness is less than the amount that they would have had to pay to dispose of the waste properly.

Just like polluters, spammers try to spread the costs of their spam across wider and wider populations of Internet users, knowing that as long as they don't give a "fatal" dose to any single Internet service provider (ISP), they can continue their spamming relatively unnoticed and everyone pays their little portion, never being the wiser or bothering to fight back.

Why Spam Is Hard to Stop

If you have ever spent an hour trying to coax, cajole, and threaten your computer into doing something it stubbornly refused to do, the following statement may come as a surprise: Simplicity is at the core of how the Internet works, especially when it comes to something as ubiquitous as e-mail. Part of what made it become so widely used is that it was easy for Internet service providers to implement and simple for software developers to program tools to use it.

At the heart of e-mail is a set of technical standards and Internet protocols that are so simple, they're called the Simple Mail Transport Protocol, or SMTP. You may have even seen the letters *SMTP* when you set up your e-mail software — it's the technology by which e-mail gets sent from a sending e-mail server at an Internet service provider (ISP) to a receiving e-mail server at another ISP. (Other protocols help you retrieve mail after it has been received at your ISP. Two of them, POP and IMAP, are in the spam-filtering chapters in Part II.)

As the popularity of the Internet grew, e-mail evolved from a novelty to a necessity. All e-mail now transmitted across the Internet is sent using the agreed-on industry standard, SMTP. Any server that "speaks" SMTP can send mail to, and receive mail from, any other server that speaks SMTP.

Because a server may be processing a dozen or more message connections per second, the SMTP "conversation" must be kept very brief. How brief? Well, before the entire e-mail message gets dumped onto a receiving server, only three pieces of information are received before the mail is delivered: the identity of the sending server, the From address, and the To address.

Thanks to lots of hard work by lots of clever people, though, you can indeed do many things to help make your inbox a cleaner and friendlier place. You can use a growing number of tools and technologies that, with some work, lots of patience, and a little luck, can make your e-mail experience much more pleasant.

Many technologies discussed in Parts II and III of this book fall into the three categories of whitelists, blacklists, and filters. For example, certain antispam services depend on turning your e-mail address book into a kind of whitelist, ensuring that you always get e-mail from those people you know. Others implement sophisticated filtering techniques, and still others use known sources of spam to create blacklists that block unwanted e-mail.

None of the technologies we discuss would qualify as a "silver bullet" to stop all spam forever, but they can definitely make a dent in the amount of spam you receive. All it takes is a strong distaste for spam and a willingness to give these new technologies a chance.

Chapter 2

How Spammers Get Your Address

● ●

In This Chapter

▶ Harvesting and scavenging from the Web

▶ Dictionary attacks

▶ Foiling attempts to grab your e-mail address

● ●

*I*f you're like most Internet users, you have had more than a few e-mail addresses over the past few years. You may have changed jobs and gotten a new e-mail address. You may have even gotten a new Internet service provider (ISP) and started using one of its e-mail accounts for your day-to-day e-mail needs. And, like many millions of people, the volumes of spam pouring into your e-mail inbox may have begun to drive you so insane that you periodically change your e-mail address just to try to stay one step ahead of the spammers.

But they found you again, didn't they?

The (depressing) reality of e-mail is that escaping spam is almost impossible. In fact, you may commonly see someone create a brand-new e-mail account and then, in the time between the moment the account is activated and the owner logs in to the account, see spam already waiting.

How does it happen? The rest of this chapter is devoted to explaining how spammers find your address and what — if anything — you can do about it.

When You're a Spammer, the World Is Your Garden

Since the first e-mail spammers began their reigns of terror over our inboxes, they got the e-mail addresses for their mailing lists by gathering them from anywhere they could. Here are some fertile fields where spammers look to find usable e-mail addresses:

- Chat rooms
- Message boards
- Usenet newsgroups
- Discussion mailing lists
- Online-service member directories
- Web pages

If an e-mail address was anywhere to be seen, spammers grabbed it and added it to their lists. Soon, the tedious task of manually scanning Web pages and chat rooms gave way to automated bots (short for ro*bots)* that systematically scoured through member directories and chat rooms on AOL, Web sites, and message boards. Everything with an @ in the middle was fair game.

The spammers call this process *address harvesting.* But the noted privacy and antispam advocate Jason Catlett, the operator of the privacy resource Web site Junkbusters.com, points out that the word *harvest* isn't accurate because it implies that you have a right to be picking something from that garden. Because spammers are usually violating ISP user agreements and loads of other rules, Catlett suggests that *poaching* is a far more appropriate term.

If you have an account on AOL, you can do a little experiment to see how efficient spammers have gotten at grabbing screen names. First, create a new screen name on your AOL account. (Each account can have as many as seven active screen names; see the AOL keyword **screen names**.) After you have created a new screen name, go to the chat rooms (AOL keyword **chat**). You're placed in a chatting "lobby" with a few dozen other chatters. Just sit there and wait for the magic words "You've got mail!"

In repeated experiments, the longest time spent in an AOL chat room before receiving e-mail spam was about 30 minutes. The shortest? Less than a minute. (And it was just e-mail spam; the Instant Message spam messages began almost as quickly.)

After you're done with the experiment, you can delete your newly created screen name. But what if you don't? Try it! Wait a few days, and then log back in to see how much spam has accumulated. Your humble co-author Ray has some AOL screen names he hasn't used for years, but keeps an eye on just for fun. One screen name hasn't been logged in to a chat room in this century, yet still averages 30 or more spams a week.

From the Yellow Pages to the Dictionary

For many years, spammers were content with just scouring chat rooms, member directories on popular chat services, and Web pages, looking for random e-mail addresses to add to their lists. Soon, however, that got to be too much trouble for our intrepid spamming brethren (and sisteren?).

Remember that spammers are in the spamming business because getting a real job would cut into their Jerry Springer–watchin' time, so anything that saves them time and effort is a special treat. Spammers have therefore found a new way to get e-mail addresses: Make them up!

The origin of the make-them-up process, or *dictionary* method, has been lost to the mists of history. But we think that it went something like this:

One day, an enterprising young spammer was sorting his voluminous e-mail address database and noticed some obvious patterns:

```
John1@aol.com
John1@hotmail.com
John1@earthlink.com
John2@aol.com
John2@hotmail.com
John2@earthlink.com
John3@aol.com
John3@hotmail.com
```

"Why couldn't I just try following those naming patterns at all the popular domain names and see whether the mail goes through?" the spammer asked himself. So, he did a little research and found out the domain names of the 50 largest Internet service providers. Then he found some Web sites that list the 50 most popular male and female first names. The spammer then plugged all that information into his database software and told the software to tack on numbers in sequence, and within a couple of hours he had a database with about 125 million e-mail addresses in it.

Perhaps not surprisingly, the *dictionary method* works well with last names too — and sports team names, cities and states, names of movie stars, names of book characters, and even random words from the dictionary!

Can 125 million e-mail addresses really be valid? Not by a long shot. Because it doesn't cost a spammer any more to send something to 124 million invalid addresses than it does to send to the 1 million valid ones he stumbled on, the waste doesn't really matter. In fact, the reality is that in sending to randomly generated addresses, enough of them got delivered to enough suckers that the spammer was able to sell enough boxes of miracle weight-loss cure to make his next layaway payment on a new pair of fuzzy dice for his 1990 Ford Festiva.

As a bonus, when John3@aol.com got tired of all the spam and signed up as John5233@hotmail.com, the spam continued flowing without a hiccup.

So, if you just opened a brand-new e-mail account and already had spam waiting the first time you logged in, you can probably blame a dictionary spammer. Even if you thought that you were being obscure when you set up the e-mail name nannygoat_snorkel@yahoo.com, it's just a matter of time before the spammer's dictionary catches up to you!

Keeping One Step Ahead of the Spammers

If it's just a matter of time before a spammer catches up to your e-mail address, is there any hope? Sure, you have some hope. But, truth be told, you can do little to completely avoid spam. What hope you have comes from taking a few basic actions to keep your e-mail address a little more low profile:

✔ **Know where your e-mail address can be found (white pages and Web pages, for example):** Do you know who has your e-mail address? Do you participate in chat rooms? Message boards? Newsgroups? Do you have your e-mail address posted on your Web page?

Try typing your e-mail address into a search engine and seeing what pops up. The answer to the age-old question of "How did those #*@%#$ get my e-mail address?" may be that you gave it to them!

✔ **Guard your primary e-mail address:** When somebody asks for your e-mail address, think twice before giving it out. Or, shield yourself behind an e-mail alias. Many ISPs allow you to create multiple e-mail addresses, which can be used for creating "sacrificial" e-mail addresses you can give out to people you're not sure you trust. For more information on creating and using e-mail aliases, see the sidebar "Dodging Spam with Mailshell," later in this chapter.

✔ **Use stand-alone e-mail software:** Most Internet browsers come bundled with e-mail programs. The problem is that by bundling the two, you may be making it easy for hackers, spammers, and unscrupulous Webmasters to get your e-mail address from your browser. For that reason, we suggest using a stand-alone e-mail product, like Eudora (www.eudora.com) or Pegasus (www.pmail.com). See Chapter 8 for information about those software packages.

✔ **Play hide-and-seek with your browser:** Even if you're using a stand-alone e-mail program, you may have at some time recorded your e-mail address somewhere within your browser, or your browser may have even grabbed it and given it away for you in an attempt to be helpful. Because the whole purpose of a browser is to share information between computers, it may be giving away that information about you to others whenever they know the right way to ask for it. If you think that your browser may be blowing the whistle on you, here's how to shut down the little snitch:

In Netscape: Choose Edit⇨Preferences from the menu bar atop the browser window. On the list along the left side of the Preferences dialog box, click the plus sign (+) next to the Mail & Newsgroups option. Then select Identity, which appears just below the plus sign. On the right side of the dialog box appears any of your personal information that the browser has stored. Erase all personal information you see there and click OK to accept the changes.

In Internet Explorer: Choose Tools⇨Internet Options from the menu bar atop the browser window. In the Internet Options dialog box, select the Content tab and click the My Profile button. Erase all personal information that appears on this form. Click OK to accept the changes.

In Opera: Choose E-Mail⇨Edit Active Account from the menu bar atop the browser window. Erase all personal information that appears in the right half of the dialog box.

✔ **Choose an ISP that actively blocks spam:** Several large national ISPs — like AOL, EarthLink, and AT&T — have some spam-blocking features, so if yours has them, make sure that you use them. Although you're likely to have more difficulty finding a local ISP that blocks spam, many are run by system administrators who are veterans of the spam wars and know how to offer spam protection that's so vigorous it makes nuclear missile silos look poorly defended. It's always worth asking around.

✔ **Find out how to filter your own e-mail:** Some e-mail software programs have filtering features that, if you take the time to read the instructions, can be useful in helping you manage your mailbox in many ways, including helping you filter spam directly into the trash. Be ready to experiment with those settings, and don't autodelete anything until you're absolutely certain that your filters are working right. If your filter eats that e-mail from Aunt Ethel, you may get a cold reception (and dinner) when you head for her house next Thanksgiving.

For more information about filtering, see Chapter 5.

Dodging spam with Mailshell

Several years ago, a clever concept in Web-based e-mail services appeared on the scene. Named Mailshell (`http://www.mailshell.com`), the concept behind it is simple: If spammers can randomly pick e-mail addresses out of thin air, why can't you?

For about $3 per month, Mailshell gives you an unlimited number of e-mail addresses and allows you to make them up instantly, without any advance preparation. For example, you may create a Mailshell account named `snidely`, whereupon you're informed that all your Mailshell e-mail addresses will end in `@snidely.mailshell.com`. You then tell Mailshell to forward all mail to your well-hidden and unguessable address, `we0ce7x9w@some-isp.com`.

Then, when you go to your local oil-change place and someone there asks for your e-mail address, you can cheerfully say "Sure! It's `Jippylube@snidely.mailshell.com`." When the oil-change place sends you e-mail to remind you that it's time for a new air filter, the mail to the Jippylube alias is quietly forwarded to your well-hidden e-mail address without the oil people ever knowing it.

As though that weren't exciting enough, there's more! If you start getting spam addressed to the Jippylube alias, you know which slimeballs sold the spammers the address! Then, when you get tired of receiving the spam sent to the Jippylube alias, you can log in to the Mailshell Web site and have it routed directly to the trash and not forwarded to you.

What if you get e-mail to a Mailshell address and you want to reply? Isn't your hidden e-mail address exposed? The clever people at Mailshell already thought of that! If you click the Reply button, the e-mail goes back to the Mailshell system, where your real e-mail address is stripped out, the alias is reinserted as the From address, and the recipient is none the wiser.

With an unlimited supply of e-mail addresses at your disposal (*disposal* is an important word here), you always know who is responsible for your spam, and you can turn it off as easily as flipping a switch.

✔ **Never** — *never* — **click Reply:** Most return addresses in spam are faked to deflect complaints. However, some spammers use real addresses because they really do want to hear from you — but not for the reason you may think. Why would they want to hear your angry diatribe? When you click Reply, you have just confirmed that your e-mail address is a live one, which is like waving a big red flag and screaming "This e-mail address is real! I really read this stuff! If you're smart, you'll send me more spam!"

✔ **Establish secondary screen names for chat rooms and message boards:** Chat rooms and message boards are among the most appealing places for spammers to gather e-mail addresses. Protect your primary e-mail address by creating other, throwaway e-mail addresses for posting on message boards and for giving out to people and sites you're not sure you can trust. Many ISPs — like AOL, AT&T, and others — allow you to create secondary screen names or additional e-mail addresses at little or no cost, or you can get free e-mail addresses from Yahoo!, Hotmail, and other free e-mail services. If spam comes flooding into those accounts, you can always delete them and make a new one, all the while shielding your primary address from the flood. For more on free e-mail services like Hotmail and Yahoo! Mail, see Chapter 10.

✔ **Give and use false e-mail addresses:** This advice is quite controversial. Many people know that spammers troll through chat rooms and message boards looking for e-mail addresses, so they use fake or altered — sometimes called *munged* (rhymes with *plunged*) — e-mail addresses. For example, `JohnDoe123@hotmail.com` may give out his address as `JohnDoe123@I-hate-spam.hotmail.com` and then give written or verbal instructions to friends and associates to remove the `I-hate-spam.` part before sending him e-mail. This strategy tends to confound many spammers because they often use automated e-mail harvesting programs that gather anything with an @ sign in the middle; because the spammers are too lazy to sort the millions of addresses by hand, they usually end up sending their spam to the altered address.

Why is munging controversial? Depending on how you munge the address, when the spammer sends the mail, it may still end up in somebody's mailbox, most likely that of the already overworked and spam-flooded administrator of your ISP or free e-mail provider. The other reason is that many people use mail programs that don't show the e-mail address of people they're writing to, so they don't notice the munge or may not even realize that it's possible that the address isn't real, and real mail gets lost. Please think twice before trying this one at home.

✔ **Use a unique e-mail account name not found in a dictionary:** Pick an e-mail address like `sdfj4k16@hotmail.com` or `qw2eru9@Yahoo.com` so that spammers are less likely to pull your e-mail address out of a hat, thin air, or the dictionary. Sure, it's difficult to remember, but see the nearby sidebar, "Dodging spam with Mailshell," for a way around that problem.

✔ **Find out how and where to complain to get spammers shut down:** The best defense is a good offense. When spammers are offending you, offend them right back by finding out how to get them booted off their ISPs. And how can you do that, you ask? Keep reading.

What More Can You Do?

Among our many suggestions, the last one in the preceding section is the hardest, but it can be the most rewarding. Among your three authors, we have helped shut down hundreds of spammers' accounts and kept them on the run. If you're ready to put a few notches in your antispam holster, turn to Chapter 4, where we teach you how to trace Internet e-mail back to its source, to find out where spammers are operating and how to get them shut down!

Chapter 3

There Oughtta Be a Law Against Spam!

● ●

In This Chapter

▶ The arguments for and against spam laws

▶ Who defines what spam is?

▶ Current U.S. and international laws

▶ Problems with enforcement

▶ What makes an effective antispam law?

● ●

Since the earliest days of the spam problem, spam victims have looked to various places for help in stopping it. When the immigration attorneys Laurence Canter and Martha Siegel let loose one of the world's first major spamming campaigns (as described in Chapter 1), the call went out for their law licenses to be stripped.

Although it took a few years (and a few more legal and ethical transgressions) for Canter and Siegel to be sent looking for another line of work, it was clear early on that people want to see spammers held legally accountable for their misbehavior. Over the next decade, consumer activists, online marketers, legislators, lawyers, lobbyists, and civil liberties experts fought over the best way to squash spammers — legally speaking.

Is Spam Already Illegal?

Many aspects of spam are already outlawed by state and federal antifraud laws and other consumer protection statutes dealing with unfair and deceptive business practices. Many products and services promoted via spam, like get-rich-quick schemes and quack medical remedies, are already illegal under existing laws. In addition, many technical tricks that spammers use to hijack e-mail servers are outlawed by state and federal computer crime statutes. Several Internet service providers (ISPs) have also successfully sued spammers under laws relating to trademark misuse and the private-property rights of network owners.

Yet many people are still calling for more laws directly targeting spam. Why? In part, because even though existing laws may outlaw lots of spam already, somebody forgot to tell the spammers. Spam volumes are still increasing, according to a September 2003 survey in *Information Week*, at a rate of 37 percent per month!

Libertarians, stop reading here!

So, if spammers are already ignoring the law, wouldn't new laws be similarly ineffective? Why bother passing new laws if the old ones aren't working? This argument is often heard from libertarian commentators.

Discussions of Internet-related legal issues invariably bring out the libertarian streak in many legal and social commentators. Most libertarians, especially those who comment on Internet issues, tend to argue that most laws are bad or irrelevant or both. These people favor letting others use technology and the power of economics and the free market to protect themselves.

Unlike the so-called liberal bias in the news media, Internet old-timers have a definite libertarian bias. That bias is the reason that nearly every news article about spam laws usually ends with some commentator saying "Of course, any effort to use laws to stop spammers is doomed to failure."

Why? The usual reasons that are given are shown in this list:

- ✔ Spammers are impossible to find because they use e-mail servers in foreign countries.

- ✔ If you do manage to find the spammers, you can never get them into court because they're in foreign countries.

✔ Even if you manage to find spammers in the United States, they just move their business off-shore and keep on spamming.

Of course, none of those reasons is true; for example:

✔ Chapter 4 shows you how easy it can be to track spammers back to the ISPs where their spam originates.

✔ Spammers can send their mail off servers in another galaxy, but as long as the spammers themselves, or the product peddlers who hire them, have some connection to the United States, U.S. laws apply.

✔ The guy selling phony Viagra out of his bedroom to earn some extra cash isn't likely to unhitch his trailer-home and drive to a Caribbean nation to avoid prosecution.

For the sake of argument, assume that spam laws would be difficult to enforce. What do the naysayers think will be the ultimate solution to the spam problem? It's the same thing that created the problem in the first place, of course: technology! Yes, technology alone can solve the spam problem, even though nearly a decade after spam became a problem, technology hasn't yet solved it.

Technology isn't the only answer

The unfortunate reality of spam is that the technology of spamming is evolving just as rapidly as the technology to stop it. In fact, the contest between spamming technology and anti-spamming technology is very much a rigged game.

The success of e-mail is due in large part to the flexibility of e-mail technology and the fundamental premise on which it is built: Make it easy and reliable for anybody to send anything to anybody. The people who invented today's e-mail protocols did a good job.

Ten years into the fight against spam, spammers are, ironically, proving in some ways that e-mail is as powerful and resilient as it is supposed to be. To prove it, spammers aren't merely using e-mail — they're abusing it in ways that are sometimes as elegant as they are obscene.

It's doubly ironic that, in an effort to save e-mail from collapsing under the weight of spammers' abuse, spam fighters are scrambling to create new technical methods of "breaking" e-mail of the flexibility that spammers exploit. It's a little like burning down the forest to stop the forest fire.

Where The Law helps all this is to act like an impartial, unbiased referee. If the game is rigged in favor of spammers, the law can step in and move the ball 10 yards closer to the goal line.

Laws can do stuff that technology can't

Laws can decide that what may be "legal" according to the rules of e-mail software is definitely not legal in the eyes of the law. And, to the best of our knowledge, no software out there can throw you in jail for ignoring a programming command.

But spam laws can also make things easier for spam victims to hold their abusers accountable in ways that technology can't. For example, in bringing a traditional lawsuit, you often have to demonstrate damages. How much damage does a single spam message cause? Very little, of course, just like a single raindrop that is harmless until it joins with billions more like it and washes you out to sea.

A law that establishes the harmful nature of spam and sets a fixed amount of damage, such as $500 per spam message, gets around the issue of trying to prove damages. It also gets around ancient judges who still think that typewriters are a little too newfangled. In some of the earliest antispam lawsuits, attorneys had to present months of arguments and evidence to even convince the judges that spam was a problem. If a law says in black and white that spam is illegal, a judge doesn't need to understand bits and bytes.

Spam: The Elusive Definition

The challenge for any effective antispam law is to truly stop spammers. One key to that goal is to define spam, although it turns out that that's easier said than done.

If you're like most people, it takes only a few seconds of reading through an e-mail message to know whether that message is spam. But whether you're programming antispam filtering technology or trying to write a law that makes spamming illegal, translating your instantaneous ability to recognize spam into a mathematical equation or a piece of legislative language is a complicated matter.

In a famous Supreme Court decision about pornography and censorship, Justice Potter Stewart recognized that defining the term *pornography* can be nearly impossible because people have differing opinions about the artistic value of a given image. But even if he couldn't define it, he famously wrote, "I know it when I see it."

How art thou spam?

Many antispam laws that have been passed in recent years have sought to define the characteristics of spam in several ways:

- ✔ **Unsolicited or solicited:** Was the message sent to someone who specifically and knowingly asked to receive that particular message? For example, is the e-mail a response to a direct inquiry, such as a request for information about a specific product, or did the recipient give the sender a business card at a booth on the floor of a convention exhibit hall and ask to be e-mailed with product information?

- ✔ **Permission or relationship:** Did the recipient of the e-mail address give permission, either expressly or in some sort of implied fashion? For example, did the recipient, while shopping online for car loan information, sign up to receive interest rate alerts from banks in the car loan business? Or does the e-mail recipient have an existing business relationship with the sender through which e-mail communications are an implied part of that relationship?

- ✔ **Commercial or noncommercial:** Does the e-mail message advertise the commercial availability of a product or service offered for sale or lease? Or is the message a solicitation for charitable contributions or promoting a political or religious cause?

✔ **Bulk or not bulk:** Was the e-mail message sent in bulk to hundreds or thousands or millions of recipients? Does it make any difference if the message was a one-time message addressed manually to just a handful of people?

✔ **E-mail or something else:** Is the message coming via e-mail or through a similar channel, such as text messaging to a cellular telephone? Does the message appear in an e-mail inbox or as a pop-up window on a computer desktop?

✔ **Forged headers:** Does the e-mail message contain any forged information, such as a false From address or a nonexistent Reply-To address? Does it have other fake addresses or falsified routing information in its headers? (For more information about e-mail headers, see Chapter 4.)

✔ **Misleading Subject lines:** Does the e-mail message try to trick the recipient into opening it by having a Subject line completely unrelated to the topic of the message? For example, does the e-mail subject say "About Your Christmas Gift Order," but the message contains an advertisement for a miracle weight-loss cure?

✔ **Fraudulent content:** Is the e-mail message advertising an illegal get-rich-quick scheme or a bogus work-from-home program or touting some unknown company whose stock is about to go through the roof?

✔ **Bogus opt-out:** Does the message offer to remove you from its mailing list, but when you click the link, the removal Web page doesn't exist? Does it direct you to reply with "unsubscribe" on the Subject line, but the e-mail bounces back saying "user unknown?" Or does clicking the Remove button net you *more* spam?

Spam is in the eye of the beholder

Here's an appalling fact: The reason spammers stay in business is that somewhere out there, somebody gets an e-mail message containing all the earmarks of spam — the forged headers, the bad Subject lines, the bogus opt-out links, the ads touting the quack medical remedy — and *buys the product anyway!*

Don't believe us? Just ask Terry Goddard — the attorney general of the state of Arizona. In 2003, his office seized from a band of crooks palatial homes, luxury cars, and piles of cash totaling more than $45 million. Their crime? Spamming advertisements for bogus creams and pills that claim to enlarge your sex organs.

All that money has been put into a restitution fund to pay back people who bought the phony cures. Perhaps not surprisingly, nobody has stepped forward to ask for their money back.

If people will spend millions on bogus remedies, they will undoubtedly spend more if the products are legitimate, no matter how they're advertised. Just look at spam's annoying cousin: telemarketing. People say that they hate telemarketing calls, yet those same people pay upward of $60 billion for goods and services each year through telemarketing.

Joining the CAUCE

In 1996, a group of antispam advocates were chatting (via e-mail, of course) about how best to tackle the growing spam problem. Many participants were technical experts working at ISPs and network administrators operating e-mail systems at major corporations. A few were also marketers who were beginning to use the Internet for legitimate electronic commerce and were horrified by the spamming ways of their fellow marketers.

Over the course of many months spent discussing various technical approaches to fighting spam, several participants came to the conclusion that spam fighters needed some legal weaponry along with their technology arsenal.

In 1997, a group of antispam activists, including two of the co-authors of this book, Ray and John, joined several other spam fighters to create an organization to fight for antispam laws. The Coalition Against Unsolicited Commercial Email (CAUCE) rapidly became the leading consumer advocacy group fighting spam, signing up tens of thousands of members in its first year of operation. Ever since, CAUCE has been educating lawmakers and influencing the debate over how best to deal with spam.

CAUCE costs nothing to join, and it doesn't ask for donations. It's an all-volunteer organization. It offers a newsletter that periodically alerts you to developments in the world of spam-related laws. To learn more, visit www.cauce.org.

For some number of people, spam isn't about whether an e-mail message delivers an advertisement in some unacceptable way, with fake addresses and bogus opt-out promises. No, for those people, the first question is "Do I want what is being advertised?"

That question is the core of why it's so hard to define spam. For some percentage of the population, the definition of spam depends on the recipient's feelings at the precise moment the e-mail message is received, and the feeling can change from one moment to the next.

If the people receiving spam can't decide what spam is, how can any technology figure it out? And how can any lawmaker write a law or regulation that can predict what will be in the minds of consumers?

The answer is that laws, like technology, can address only a part of the spam problem. Despite the difficult hurdles, lawmakers in many states across the United States, and indeed in many countries around the world, have tried to do their part, with varying levels of success.

Current Laws on Spam

First, a disclaimer: At the time this chapter was being written, in late 2003, 35 states had antispam laws, but no federal antispam law had yet been passed. In the waning days of his governorship of California, Gray Davis signed into law the repeal of a weak antispam law and replaced it with one of the strongest antispam laws in the United States. Yet, just a few weeks later, the United States Senate passed a bill that, if signed into law as written, would render California's new law — and every other state antispam law — unenforceable.

Why the flurry of activity? In part, the volume of spam in the first half of 2003 had skyrocketed past the dizzying heights of previous years. By September 2003, *InformationWeek* magazine was projecting a 400 percent increase in spam volume over the previous year's volumes. These huge numbers finally caught lawmakers' attention and suggested that the laws that had been enacted over the preceding six years or so weren't working.

State-by-state

A number of states have passed antispam laws, with varying provisions, definitions, and penalties. The most frequent provisions in those laws are shown in this list:

- **Opt-in or opt-out options:** *Opt-in* laws generally require that senders have the permission, either express or implied through a business relationship, to send e-mail to recipients. *Opt-out* laws allow senders to send e-mail without permission, but typically permit recipients to ask to be removed.

- **ADV or ADLT labels:** Several state laws require commercial e-mail to be labeled with some variation of the letters *ADV* on the Subject line, and in some cases *ADLT* if the e-mail is of a sexual or pornographic nature.

- **No false routing:** Many laws prohibit the use of forged or falsified routing information.

- **No misleading subject:** Several state laws prohibit the use of a misleading Subject line designed to trick recipients into opening a message.

- **Valid opt-out options:** Several laws require each commercial e-mail message to contain some type of instructions telling recipients how to get off future mailings by that company and requiring companies to obey consumers' opt-out requests.

- **Contact info:** Many laws require that a company sending an e-mail provide the company's name and a physical address or other contact information.

- **No using third party's domain name:** Several laws specifically forbid using anybody else's domain name to send spam without their permission. This type of law curtails the harm inflicted on innocent third parties who may be flooded with complaints or rejected e-mails.

Spam around the world

Although the United States Congress is still bickering over antispam laws, governments around the world have been quicker to take action. In the European Union (EU), a new law banning all unsolicited commercial e-mail took effect in 2002 and required all member nations of the EU to enact similar laws before October 31, 2003, which they all did.

Huge spam problems in South Korea drove its Parliament to enact an antispam law in 2002. However, the first attempt was an opt-out law, which permitted spammers to send as much e-mail as they wanted, as long as recipients were given an opportunity to opt out of future e-mails. After spam volumes skyrocketed, the South Korean government amended the law to take an opt-in approach and added stiffer criminal penalties. According to the government agency in charge of telecommunications, Korean spam volumes are slowly coming down.

As of late 2003, antispam laws were also being considered in Canada, Australia, and even, reportedly, China. Antispam efforts are also being considered in other countries where the spam problem has gotten out of hand, such as Japan, Taiwan, Brazil, and a few other nations.

How to Make Spam Laws Work

Enforcing antispam laws ain't easy, starting with the question of who is allowed to do the enforcement. Many state antispam laws leave enforcement up to the state's attorney general. This same attorney general is also chasing bank robbers, kidnappers, and Enron executives and is maybe fighting over a Ten Commandments statue. This person already has an awfully crowded list of people to sue or throw in jail, and spammers may be pretty far down the list. (Frankly, we're glad that they're busy with those other tasks. We hate spam, but we hate kidnappers much more.)

Similarly, many antispam proposals depend on a federal agency, such as the Federal Trade Commission (FTC), to enforce the law. The FTC has excellent lawyers and investigators who are really good at big lawsuits against multimillion-dollar organizations that hide their ill-gotten proceeds in Swiss bank accounts. But asking the FTC to police day-to-day spam problems is like calling in the Army to keep your neighbor's dog from digging up your yard. The FTC may be able to muster the resources to sue the 10 biggest spammers, but it has no prayer of stopping the hundreds or thousands of small-time spammers.

Many state laws also give ISPs the right to bring lawsuits against spammers. ISPs already have at their disposal some legal tools to sue spammers: trademark, trespass, and computer crime laws. Some ISPs have used these laws to shut down some big spammers.

But in the last decade, ISPs have brought only a few dozen lawsuits against spammers. Why? Because bringing a lawsuit in federal court can cost lots of money. Spending $250,000 on a lawsuit that recovers $50,000 in damages is quite common. As a result, only the biggest ISPs can afford to bring these types of lawsuits.

So how do you make an antispam law enforceable and effective? You give the people — those of us who suffer with spam every day — the right to fight back.

Power to the People!

When average citizens are being spammed into oblivion, a time-tested method of helping to protect them is to give them the tools to defend themselves. Hundreds of state and federal laws grant individuals the ability to walk down to their local small claims court and sue the pants off whoever is bothering them. This practice is such a part of our culture that our television listings had, at last count, a dozen small claims court-type television shows. (We're not counting "Fashion Court" on the Style Channel, where people sue their friends for crimes against good taste.)

Consumers can sue spammers too. The Telephone Consumer Protection Act of 1991, for example, gives everyone the ability to sue telemarketers who all too often break many of the detailed laws relating to telemarketing. The same law allows recipients of unsolicited fax advertisements to sue fax spammers for between $500 and $1,500 per fax! (To find out more about suing faxers and rampant telemarketers, pick up a copy of *Internet Privacy For Dummies*, by John R. Levine, Ray Everett-Church, Gregg Stebben, and David Lawrence. It's another fine book by Wiley Publishing, Inc.)

It took only a few dozen lawsuits in small claims courts around the nation to all but destroy the junk faxing industry. No federal agencies or attorneys general were required! The spam crisis is tailor-made for the kind of self-help that only a few laws across the United States give average citizens.

Why don't more laws give consumers the right to sue spammers? The sad truth is that many legislators have a hatred for trial lawyers that blinds them to the idea that giving individuals a right to sue may be effective. Even the staunchest anti–Big Government representatives in Congress seem to be more willing to hire an army of new government lawyers than to let a platoon of consumers run to small claims court.

If you think that the fear of trial lawyers is irrational, we agree. The record shows that the vast majority of junk fax lawsuits were brought by small plaintiffs, not by teams of ambulance chasers assembling class action suits that tie up legitimate companies in court for decades.

Never mind that the solutions to those fears are easily written into any spam law. For example, if lawmakers fear that an antispam law may generate a flood of litigation, they can easily enough forbid class action suits or restrict lawsuits to small claims courts, where lawyers are usually prohibited from practicing.

The Future of Antispam Laws

The antispam legal world is constantly changing. In the few months after this book was published, a federal law dealing with spam may well have been signed into law. If so, Congress may well have chosen to repeat many of the same mistakes committed by many states and even a few other countries in passing a law that doesn't completely ban spam. If Congress chooses not to ban spam, then no matter when you read this book, you may still receive plenty of spam in your mailbox.

The reality of any antispam law is that it is only as effective as the lawmakers who write it decide that it should be. So, if you're not impressed with the current state of your e-mail inbox, the most important thing you can do is to let your elected officials know that whatever they have done — or haven't done, as the case may be — is simply unacceptable.

At the end of the day, your elected officials work for you, and as much as they may hate spammers (or even trial lawyers), they would hate losing their jobs even more!

Chapter 4

Talk to the Hand 'Cuz the Spammer Don't Care

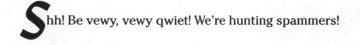

In This Chapter

▶ Deciphering e-mail headers

▶ Finding the spammer's ISP

▶ How to complain about spam

▶ How not to complain about spam

Shh! Be vewy, vewy qwiet! We're hunting spammers!

Ask Elmer Fudd and he'll tell you that hunting spammers is much like hunting wabbits. Wid a wabbit, the first place you look is in his hole, even though you know that you'll never find him there. With a spammer, the first place you look is at the From line of his spam message. Just like wid a wascally wabbit, though, you know that you'll never find him there.

Indeed, 99.99 percent of the time, the From line in a spam message is fabricated and has nothing to do with the spam's source. This trick is just one that spammers use to try to keep you off their trail. After you learn the ropes, however, hunting down a spammer's base of operations and getting him booted off the Internet is usually a cinch.

Tracking and complaining about spammers is a pretty technical process, but it's not hard after you get the hang of it. Most people don't want to bother spending the time to send complaints, especially people who receive dozens of spam messages a day; if we all do our part, however, we can reduce the amount of spam that flows.

Look at E-Mail Headers

Like a piece of luggage on an airline, every e-mail message has attached to it a little tag containing data that tells you where it started, where it has been, and what its ultimate destination was. In e-mail messages, this data is contained in a block of text called the *header,* which looks something like this:

```
Return-Path: <hptimeline@yahoo.com>
Received: from ns.isoutsider.com (unknown
[210.109.171.2]) by receiving.my-isp.com
(8.9.3/8.9.3) with ESMTP id FSW930923; Sun, 31 Aug
2003 22:59:28 -0700 (PDT)
Received: from adventures (CPE-
65-31-127-1.wi.rr.com [65.31.127.1]) by
ns.isoutsider.com (8.11.6/8.11.6) with ESMTP id
h7JFLKK09863; Sun, 31 Aug 2003 22:56:22 +0900
Message-Id:
<200308191.h7JK09867@ns.isoutsider.com>
Received: from billclinton.whitehouse.gov
([184.325.23.124]) by mailout.yahooo.com (Postfix)
with SMTP id 7600A32641; Sun, 31 Aug 2003 11:40:44
-0700 (PDT)
From: hptimeline@yahoo.com
To: <Undisclosed.Recipients>
Subject: Look Great for the Spring with Discounts
on HGH (human growth hormone)!!!!!
Date: Sat, 30 Aug 2003 02:10:21 -0800
MIME-Version: 1.0
Reply-To: hptimeline@yahoo.com
Errors-To: pow@163.com
```

Because most e-mail software creators think that average users would be terrified (or bored) by all this gobbledygook, most e-mail programs hide headers so that you never see them. Headers are the keys to finding spammers, though, so we tell you how to ferret out headers from most popular e-mail programs.

First, open the offending e-mail message; to view the e-mail header, you may need to open it in its own window. Then follow the instructions for your e-mail program:

✔ **The Unix programs Elm, Pine, and Mutt:** Press **h** to turn on the display of full headers.

✔ **Eudora:** Under the title bar are four option buttons. The third one from the left is a box that says Blah, Blah, Blah. (We are not making this up.) Select that box to display the full headers.

✔ **Hotmail:** Choose Options⇨Preferences⇨Message Headers from the menu bar. Then select the Full option to display Received headers. Selecting the Advanced option displays the MIME headers, but those usually aren't necessary for spam hunting.

✔ **Lotus Notes 4.6.x:** Choose Actions⇨Delivery Information. Then cut and paste the text from the bottom box, marked Delivery Information.

✔ **Netscape WebMail:** In the yellow field atop the message (where the Subject, Date, From, and To information appears), look for a small, yellow down arrow in the lower-right corner. Click the arrow to open the yellow field and display the full headers.

✔ **Netscape 4.x and 7.1 and Mozilla Mail:** Choose View⇨Headers⇨All.

✔ **Outlook Express:** Choose File⇨Properties and click the Details tab. If you're filing a complaint, save some time by clicking the Message Source button, which opens a text window with the full headers and full plain-text message body displayed. (Spam investigators benefit from having everything in plain text rather than with colorful fonts and other elements.)

✔ **Outlook 2000, 2002, and 2003:** Choose View⇨Options. You see the message headers in a box at the bottom of the Message Options window. You can copy or paste them from that window.

✔ **Pegasus Mail:** Choose Reader⇨Show All Headers. (You can choose the same command by pressing Ctrl+H instead.)

Follow the flow of Received headers

Every time an e-mail message passes through a mail server, that system adds a Received line. Although lots of extraneous data is on these Received lines, they're simple enough to read: The mail was received from one computer by another computer at a certain date and time. Each new Received line gets added to the top of the pile, so the most recent one should be the one that says who delivered it to your ISP.

The key pieces of information contained in every block of headers is the IP address. An *Internet Protocol (IP) address* is a unique numerical address, represented as a series of numbers separated by "dots" (such as 192.168.128.3). Every computer that connects to the Internet gets an IP address because that's how every other computer on the Internet knows, for example, which computer is requesting to view a Web page and where to send the data that is being requested.

Whenever a computer is connected to the Internet, it's assigned an IP address number from a pool of numbers that were allocated to that ISP by the people in charge of numbers on the Internet (read more about these "people" later in this chapter, in the section "Don't complain to IANA!"). If you can find a legitimate IP address in an e-mail header, you can often trace the address back to the ISP to which that number was assigned and use it to send a complaint. The trick is to find which numbers you can trust and which are there to throw you off the trail.

In this example, the first Received line is the latest one, and relevant pieces of data are shown in bold:

```
Received: from ns.isoutsider.com (unknown
[210.109.171.2]) by receiving.my-isp.com
(8.9.3/8.9.3) with ESMTP id FSW930923; Sun, 31 Aug
2003 22:59:28 -0700 (PDT)
```

This line says that the mail was received by the ISP (my-isp.com) from ns.isoutsider.com, which has the IP address 210.109.171.2. Because you can be confident that your own ISP isn't sending you spam, you now have the computer named ns.isoutsider.com in your sight. Don't stop looking there! You can look at the next Received line to see whether the trail goes any further:

```
Received: from adventures (CPE-
65-31-127-1.wi.rr.com [65.31.127.1]) by
ns.isoutsider.com (8.11.6/8.11.6) with ESMTP id
h7JFLKK09863; Sun, 31 Aug 2003 22:56:22 +0900
```

Sure enough, the trail continues. According to the next Received line, somebody gave this spam to ns.isoutsider.com — namely, a computer that calls itself adventures. It seems, however, that your new friend adventures is a little confused about its name. You see, when the computer ns.isoutsider.com received the message, it performed a lookup and found the *real* name of adventures and added it to the Received header. The real name of adventures appears to be CPE-65-31-127-1.wi. rr.com. (We talk more about that lookup thing in the sidebar "Nslookup in a nutshell," later in this chapter.) Whatever its name really is, adventures is now your prime suspect. Keep going!

On the next Received line, you see:

```
Received: from billclinton.whitehouse.gov
([184.325.23.124]) by mailout.yahooo.com (Postfix)
with SMTP id 7600A32641; Sun, 31 Aug 2003 11:40:44
-0700 (PDT)
```

If some things about this line look funny to you, you're right. First, you know that Bill gave the White House back a few years ago to the same family he got it from. Second, you're pretty sure that the folks at the White House have better things to do than send you spam. Third, another domain in there, yahooo.com, looks suspiciously like somebody didn't know how to spell *yahoo* correctly. Combined, these issues raise some real questions about the legitimacy of this Received line.

On top of all that, it turns out that something is wrong with Bill's IP address. It breaks a rule that's called, for simplicity's sake, "the 255 rule." This rule says that the numbers in IP addresses are never, *never*, outside the range from 0 through 255. (If you want to understand why, see the following sidebar, "An explanation of the 255 rule.") In the IP address 184.325. 23.124, the second number (325) is too big to be true. That the second number breaks the 255 rule means that this IP address is bogus. Coupling that information with the unlikely computer name, you seem to have reached a dead end. That leaves you with adventures, also known as CPE-65-31-127- 1.wi.rr.com, as the end of the trail.

An explanation of the 255 rule

You don't need to know this rule to be able to track down spam, but because you're here anyway, we explain it. People, most of whom have 10 fingers, prefer to count in base 10; computers, which have, at most, 2 fingers, prefer to count in base 2, which uses only the digits 0 and 1. An IP address is really a 32-digit base 2 number (usually referred to as 32 bits). The IP address for our Web site, at www.privacyfordummies.com, is

11010000000111110010101
001100111

Even for us computer weenies, that kind of number is a bit challenging to remember, so we divide the number into four 8-bit chunks:

11010000.00011111.00101
010.01100111

Then we treat each 8-bit chunk as a number and translate it into its base 10 equivalent:

208.31.42.103

The smallest value that an 8-bit chunk can contain is 00000000, which is 0 in base 10, and the largest is 11111111, which is 255. A number less than 0 or greater than 255, therefore, can't be translated back into an 8-bit number and can't be part of an IP address.

What happens, though, if the last Received line doesn't have any funny-looking names or has an IP address that doesn't violate the 255 rule? What if you see several more Received lines? Then you keep following the Received lines backward until you find one that doesn't link up with the one before it.

Look up the owner of the last verifiable mail-handling server

Suppose that after reviewing the message headers, you have collected the following computer names and IP addresses that you suspect of being involved in sending you spam:

```
ns.isoutsider.com (210.109.171.2)
CPE-65-31-127-1.wi.rr.com (65.31.127.1)
billclinton.whitehouse.gov (184.325.23.124)
```

(For the moment, suppose that you don't know anything about the 255 rule and that you have no reason to doubt the existence of a computer named `billclinton.whitehouse.gov`.) Now is the time to put the power of the Internet to work to start tracking down the spammer. You can use the nslookup tool, which enables you to find out whether these computer names and IP addresses match each other. To use nslookup, go to one of the Web-based nslookup services (try the one at `www.samspade.org/t`), find the "address digger" field, and type the name of each computer (for example, **ns.isoutsider.com**). You see something like this:

```
ns.isoutsider.com resolves to 210.109.171.2
CPE-65-31-127-1.wi.rr.com resolves to 65.31.127.1
Error - billclinton.whitehouse.gov doesn't exist
```

Because nslookup can find those first two IP addresses and they appear to be the same as the names indicated in the headers, you can be fairly confident that they're accurately represented. If you see a discrepancy, try plugging in the number to see whether nslookup can find a name. This process of putting in a number, getting a name, and then putting in a name and getting a number, is referred to as doing *forward* and *reverse* lookups. When in doubt, we usually trust numbers over names because sometimes the same server may answer to many names.

Because the last address appears to be fake, you can't track down its owner. The last verifiable mail handler on the trail of addresses is `rr.com` — which is the domain name for RoadRunner, the high-speed cable modem service owned by Time Warner — address at `CPE-65-31-127-1.wi.rr.com`.

Nslookup in a nutshell

All computers connected to the Internet are assigned a unique numerical address, the *IP address*. In addition, many (but not all) computers are assigned names that are more easily remembered by humans. So, rather than remember `192.168.123.45`, you have to remember only `www.some-crazy-website`.

`com`, and the Internet's *domain name system* (DNS) translates the names into numbers for you. When you have a number but no name, or a name but no number, the program nslookup (also known as *name system lookup*) does a reverse lookup for you and gets you what you need.

Investigate the Contents of the Spam

You should remember that you don't want to just stop spammers at the source of the spam — you also want to shut down the operation advertised in the spam. Otherwise, the spammer just moves to some other ISP and keeps on spamming. You're aided in this effort by the fact that most ISPs forbid their customers to spam — from anywhere — to advertise activities hosted on their network. Thus, even if a spammer is using a UUNet dial-up to send out spam that advertises a Web site being hosted by someone else, both UUNet and the site hosting the Web site may give the spammer the boot. You should look in the text of the spam message for any identifiable information or clues, such as an e-mail address or a Web address.

Suppose that the spammer's message contains the following text:

```
Wholesale Prescription Medications
DISCREET OVERNIGHT PHARMACY!

Now get HGH, Vicodin, Sex Organ Enhancements,
Prozac, Viagr@, BustPro, Zoloft, Propecia. And
many, many more!
Just e-mail doctorfeelgood328@yahoo.com, or visit
our web site at
http://1024349897/HGH_13/specialoffer.html
```

In this example, the spammer is using a maildrop at Yahoo.com and is hosting a Web site. (A *maildrop* is the e-mail equivalent of a post office box — it's easy to set up and provides a good bit of anonymity if trouble arises.) But the Web page address looks a little strange. The domain name isn't the usual www, and it's not an IP address in the form you would recognize from your research. In this case, the spammer is using an obscure trick to mask the IP address. Luckily, most nslookup tools can see right through the subterfuge: Plugging 1024349897 into the Obfuscated URL tool at www.samspade. org/t tells you that it translates into 61.14.86.201, for which further lookups reach a translation into c201. h061014086.is.net.tw.

Get Ready to Address Your Complaints

After you have identified all the sites a spam message is coming from, it's time to figure out how and where to file complaints. Luckily, if you look carefully on an ISP's Web site, you often find information about its *terms of service,* or the rules by which all its subscribers agree to abide. In many cases, ISPs prohibit any form of spam-related activity that they can think of and even give you an address for filing complaints.

The most common complaint address is abuse@ followed by the domain name. Indeed, most respectable ISPs maintain an abuse address for their domains. In some cases, however, you may have to use a fallback address: postmaster@this-darn-spammers-ISP.com. Although not every ISP is bright enough to operate an abuse address, Internet e-mail protocols require that any entity providing mail service for a domain maintain a functioning postmaster account and that the account be read regularly by a human being. Therefore, your default complaint addresses usually are abuse@ or postmaster@ at the domain in question. This method is really hit-or-miss, though, because the domain names aren't always where mail for those domains is supposed to be sent.

Signing up for Abuse.net service

You can use abuse.net in two different ways: Ask it to forward your mail to the appropriate place or ask it what the appropriate place is and mail it yourself.

The second way is easier: Point your browser at www.abuse.net/look up.phtml, type the domain in the box on that page, and click the Lookup button. You see the list of addresses to use.

To use the mail forwarder, you have to register first. To do that, send a blank message to new@abuse.net. You should shortly get back a confirmation with the Abuse.net terms of service. Read the terms, and if you agree to them (mostly, you agree not to use Abuse.net to harass people), follow the instructions in that message to send back a message indicating your agreement. After you have done that, you can just send your complaint to addresses like example.com@abuse.net, and it automatically forwards the message as best it can.

Do-it-yourself IP address deciphering

So you want to be a Sherlock Holmes or Mike Hammer and learn to track down the owner of the spam Web site or IP address yourself? There's really not much to it, thanks to some handy Web-based tools, available for free over the Internet. Here's how to do it:

Browse to `www.geektools.com/whois.php` and plug the IP address into the whois tool. (No, we're not kidding about the name, and the tool does exactly as its name implies: It tells you "whois" responsible for the IP address.)

When you plug `61.14.86.201` into whois, you get a long listing, part of which includes this information:

```
Checking server
   [whois.twnic.net.tw]
Results:
Registrant:
   Infoserve Technology
   Corp.
   11F, No.105, Sec.2,
   Tun-Hua S. Rd.,
   Taipei, Taiwan
   TW
```

```
Domain Name: is.net.tw
Contact:
   Johnny Liu
   johnnyl@infoserve.co
   m.tw
   TEL: 02-2325-2060
   #102
   FAX: 02-2325-2566
```

What all this means is that the contact person for that IP address is an administrator at an ISP in Taiwan. Although you can send your complaint to that person, you probably should try the abuse and postmaster addresses first. You don't want to send complaints to the administrator's personal mailbox unless you have to.

If whois doesn't like the spammer-obscured URL, you may need to use the nslookup or traceroute programs to convert the `1024349897` into `61.14.86.201` and then try plugging the regular IP address back into whois.

In truth, the best way to find the right address to send your spam complaint is to sign up for our very own John Levine's Abuse.net forwarding service. (Don't worry: It's free! See the nearby sidebar "Signing up for Abuse.net service.") The service forwards along your complaint for you. After you sign up for Abuse.net, you just address your complaint to the domain name shown in the spam (for example, `CPE-65-31-127-1.wi.rr.com`) and add `@abuse.net` at the end, and Abuse.net figures out the rest. How does it do that? It tries mixing and matching different parts of the domain and then looks them up in a big database that John maintains when he should be writing books. You can send your complaint to `rr.com` by addressing it to

```
CPE-65-31-127-1.wi.rr.com@abuse.net
```

Alternatively, visit `www.abuse.net/lookup.phtml` to see what addresses Abuse.net recommends for any domain of interest (no registration needed).

If you don't use Abuse.net, your complaint addresses are likely to be

```
abuse@isoutsider.com
abuse@rr.com
abuse@yahoo.com
abuse@is.net.tw
```

(Or, you can use `postmaster` in place of `abuse`.) If you do use Abuse.net, your complaint addresses are

```
ns.isoutsider.com@abuse.net
CPE-65-31-127-1.wi.rr.com@abuse.net
yahoo.com@abuse.net
c201.h061014086.is.net.tw@abuse.net
```

Send Your Complaints — Nicely

Don't transfer your anger at a spammer to the ISP. In most cases, it's just as angry about the spammer as you are, and although an ISP should be pleased to receive your complaint so that it can justify booting the spammer off the network, the spam really isn't the ISP's fault. Just state your case plainly. Here's a good example:

> Dear Administrator:
>
> I received a piece of spam that I have attached below. The headers appear to have originated at RoadRunner and been relayed via `ns.is outsider.com`, and it advertises both a mailbox at Yahoo.com and a Web page at `is.net. tw`. Please take appropriate action to stop this spammer. Thanks!

Don't fight spam with spam

One of the most common tricks spammers use to hide their whereabouts is to relay their messages off the mail server of an innocent third party. This tactic *doubles* the damage because now both the receiving system and the innocent relay system are flooded with junk e-mail. For any mail that gets through, many times the flood of complaints goes back to the innocent site because it was made to look like the origin of the spam. Another common trick is to forge the headers of messages, making it appear that the message originated elsewhere, again providing a convenient target for the anger of recipients and the flood of complaints. This is why we point out this information to you: If an ISP claims innocence, don't fight back with more complaints. It really may be innocent.

Make sure that you attach a complete copy of the spam, including all headers just as you received them. The ISP wants to do its own investigation and, without the headers, doesn't have anything concrete to work with. If you're using e-mail software that allows you to send e-mail using HTML or RTF formatting (bold or colored text or embedded pictures, for example), turn those options off and send your message in plain text because those formatting features can make it difficult to read the headers and contents of the spam.

If your research is good and you were able to locate the correct addresses for filing complaints, you're likely to receive confirmations from some ISPs stating that they received your mail and plan to take action. Don't be surprised if you don't receive anything more than this initial acknowledgement, however. Most abuse departments are overworked and understaffed; in the time it would take them to send you a personal note to thank you and pat you on the back and let you know what became of your complaint, they could have killed a few more spammer accounts.

Likewise, don't be surprised if some of your complaints bounce back to you as undeliverable. With all due respect to the many fine network administrators around the world, it's not at all uncommon for non-U.S. ISPs and corporations to be completely ill prepared to deal with spammers and to even be poorly informed about basic Internet protocols, such as the one requiring the `postmaster@` address. You should give them the benefit of the doubt, but you may need to try some whois inquiries to see whether you can locate additional addresses to which complaints can be sent. Meanwhile, many countries that are relatively new to the Internet are lousy when it comes to cleaning up messes caused by spammers. Unfortunately, spammers know this information, so they like to relay their spam off sites in countries like Japan, China, Korea, and India and in Central Europe.

When complaints bounce back, go upstream

If your complaints are bouncing back and the spam is still flowing, it's time to play hardball. Sometimes, ISPs aren't as enlightened about the problems created by spammers, but the good news is that the company that sells the ISP its Internet connection is probably a bit more spam-savvy. Suppose that your new friend Infoserve in Taiwan (the company to whom you complained so nicely) hasn't clamped down on the spammers and your complaints are falling on deaf ears. You still have some recourse because when data travels from one computer to another on the Internet, the bits of data follow a path, hopping from computer to computer between the origin and the destination. So you can use another tool in your Internet toolkit, traceroute, to find out where the spammer is getting his Internet connection. *Traceroute* traces the route (surprise!) of messages from one Internet server to another.

You can use traceroute by surfing to `www.geektools.com` and choosing Traceroute from the menu at the top. When you choose traceroute, you're presented with a long list of traceroute sites, which is good because by tracing from different places around the world, you can get a more accurate picture of who a site's upstream provider is.

Another good traceroute choice is `www.tracert.com/cgi-bin/trace.pl`, which lets you automatically select several places around the world to trace from. Running a trace on `61.14.86.201` yields variations on the following output:

```
traceroute to 61.14.86.201 (61.14.86.201), 30 hops
max, 40 byte packets
 1 inside.fw1.sjc2.mfnx.net (208.184.213.129)
 2 99.ge-5-1-1.er10a.sjc2.us.above.net
(64.124.216.10) 2.146 ms
 3 so-2-0-0.mpr3.sjc2.us.above.net (64.125.30.89)
0.788 ms
 4 pos5-0.mpr1.pao1.us.above.net (208.184.233.142)
0.894 ms
 5 134.159.63.249 (134.159.63.249) 0.880 ms
 6 i-13-0.wil-core01.net.reach.com (202.84.143.61)
13.073 ms
 7 i-3-3.tmhstcbr01.net.reach.com (202.84.143.214)
180.561 ms
 8 i-6-2.ntp-core01.net.reach.com (202.84.144.70)
211.031 ms
 9 i-1-1.ntp01.net.reach.com (202.84.180.142)
211.333 ms
10 202.148.160.18 (202.148.160.18) 217.202 ms
11 192.168.253.38 (192.168.253.38) 216.497 ms
12 * * *
```

Because everybody traces from different places, the results start out differently; in the end, though, they all seem to go through the same place: a sequence of machines at Reach. com and then to a machine numbered 202.148.160.18 and then to one numbered 192.168.253.38, and then the trail goes cold.

Doing a whois lookup on 202.148.160.18 tells you that the contact for it is Infoserve Operations, which is probably the same Infoserve that gave you the cold shoulder earlier. This information would seem to suggest that is.net.tw is connected via Reach.com. You have no guarantee, but it's a good bet that a complaint to Reach.com may get to someone who knows how to crack some heads at Infoserve.

You could also try doing a whois lookup on 192.168.253.38 (the last computer listed in the traceroute results), but it returns a strange response that says, in part:

```
OrgName: Internet Assigned Numbers Authority
OrgID: IANA
Address: 4676 Admiralty Way, Suite 330
City: Marina del Rey
StateProv: CA
PostalCode: 90292-6695
Country: US
```

```
NetRange: 192.168.0.0 - 192.168.255.255
CIDR: 192.168.0.0/16
NetType: IANA Special Use
Comment: This block is reserved for special
purposes.
Comment: Please see RFC 1918 for additional
information.
```

Don't complain to IANA!

Earlier in this chapter, while discussing how IP addresses work, we referred to the "people who are in charge of numbers on the Internet." The Internet Assigned Numbers Authority (IANA) is the outfit that doles out IP addresses. They have a few blocks of numbers, such as the block of numbers running from 192.168.0.0 to 192.168.255.255, that are reserved for use in special circumstances.

One such circumstance is for use inside a corporation's internal network. This is likely what's happening in our earlier traceroute example; the trace function reached the internal boundary of the Infoserve network, which is a machine that claims to be 192.168.253.38. For security reasons, many organizations don't allow traceroutes to go any further than that outer boundary, and that's probably why the traceroute path went cold.

So don't complain to IANA about spam when you run across somebody with an IP address that whois says belongs to it! Those numbers are reserved for anybody to use inside the confines of its network, and the IANA doesn't have any control over how they're used. You can learn more about IANA at www.iana.net.

When All Else Fails, Tell It To Your ISP

If nothing else is working, you should send documentation of your efforts to your ISP and ask it to block the spamming sites at their routers. If the ISP isn't responsive, take your business to an ISP that is prepared to give you the service you deserve.

Part II
Filtering Spam Out of Your Inbox

The 5th Wave   By Rich Tennant

"He saw your laptop and wants to know if he can check his Hotmail account to clean out his spam."

In this part . . .

Spam is here to stay, at least for now. But even though spam may continue to fly around the Internet for years to come, you don't have to read it, or even see it. This part of the book describes the features of the major e-mail programs — Outlook, Outlook Express, Netscape, Mozilla, Eudora, Pegasus, AOL, AOL Communicator — in addition to the major Web-based mail systems — Hotmail, MSN, and Yahoo! Mail.

Chapter 5

Mailbox Filtering in Your E-Mail Program

In This Chapter

▶ Letting your e-mail program do the sorting with filters

▶ Making mail folders and mailboxes in which to sort mail

▶ Determining which e-mail program you use

▶ Creating filters that catch spam (or everything *except* spam)

▶ A round-up of e-mail programs

. . . .

*W*hen your e-mail program gets your mail, it arrives in your inbox. With paper mail, you probably sort your letters into categories including junk mail, bills, magazines, and letters from real human beings. You can do the same thing with your e-mail: Rather than leave all unread messages in your inbox, you can move them to mail folders with names like Newsletters and Messages from Fred. For spam, you can move the messages directly into your Trash folder.

This chapter describes how mail folders work and how you can create *filters,* which tell your e-mail program to sort incoming messages into your folders — it's like having your own secretary. (You still have to fetch your own coffee, though.) The rest of the chapters in this section detail the exact steps to follow, depending on which e-mail program you're using. (If you're not sure, see the section "Which E-Mail Program Do You Use?" at the end of this chapter.)

If you don't know how to use your e-mail program to send and receive messages, pick up a copy of *The Internet For Dummies*, by John R. Levine, Carol Baroudi, and Margaret Levine Young (Wiley Publishing, Inc.).

Filters and folders, by themselves, don't do a good job against spam because spammers change the text of their messages faster than anyone can create filters. However, filters work hand in hand with many of the spam-filtering programs described in Part III.

Where Messages Live: Mail Folders and Mailboxes

Most e-mail programs come with a set of folders in which your messages are stored, including folders like these:

- **Inbox:** Stores incoming messages.

- **Outbox:** Stores outgoing messages. Some e-mail programs move messages to a Sent Items folder after they have been sent over the Internet.

- **Deleted Items or Trash:** Stores stuff you have deleted. To get rid of the messages completely, you give a command to empty the trash.

You can create your own folders too, with names like these:

- **Personal:** Stores stuff that has nothing to do with your work and that you probably shouldn't even be sending or receiving from this computer, but what the heck.

- **To Do:** Stores messages on which you really ought to take some kind of action one of these days — maybe tomorrow.

- **Budget:** Stores all those endless memos that circulate after each endless budget meeting, but that you need to keep for when you need to update your department's budget.

Okay, those may not be the extra folders you would find useful, but you get the general idea: You can create folders for topics about which you want to save messages.

If you subscribe to e-mail mailing lists — whether they're newsletter-style announcement lists or anyone-can-talk discussion lists — consider creating a mail folder for each mailing list. Your e-mail program can then move your mailing list messages to that folder so that you can read them separately from the rest of your messages. You can also make a folder for certain correspondents so that you can file in one place all mail from your mother-in-law, for example. (See how handy the Trash folder can be?)

Moving Your Messages with Filters

A *filter* tells your e-mail program to move specific incoming messages from your inbox to another folder. Not all e-mail programs include filters, but most do. You create a filter by telling the program two things:

- ✔ **Which messages you want to move:** You identify the part of the message to look in (the To address, From address, Subject line, or body of the message) and the word or phrase to look for. If your e-mail program finds the text, the filter takes action!

- ✔ **Where to move the messages:** You specify the name of the mail folder to move the message to.

If your e-mail program lets you create filters, you can create as many filters as you want (within reason). Considering how many different kinds of spam are out there, that's a good thing!

For example, you can create a filter that moves all messages that have the From address vpcorpfinance@megacorp.com into your Messages From Mom folder. You can create other filters that move your *New York Times*, CNN, and other daily news reports to a News folder, identifying them by their From addresses or by words or phrases that always appear on their Subject lines. Most important, you can create lots of spam filters that dump them directly to the trash.

Identifying Spam for Filtering

The key to using filters to get rid of spam is identifying which messages to move to your Trash or Deleted Items folder. Here are some ideas for useful spam filters:

✔ **Drug names or body parts mentioned on the Subject line:** If the Subject header of the message contains *Viagra* or *enhancement* or mentions body parts that we don't usually discuss in polite conversation, chances are that it's spam. We have been known to include phrases like *adult webcam* and *orgasm* in our spam filters too.

✔ **Classic spam Subject lines:** Messages with subjects containing the phrases *cartridge prices, mass mailer,* or *get out of debt* are certainly spam.

✔ **Domain names of known spammers:** If messages from specific organizations annoy you, select for trashing all messages where the From address ends in that domain name (for example, `manhood-enhancement.com`).

✔ **Bogus user name:** Spammers sometimes send messages with the From address `friend@somedomain.com`, which aren't likely to be from a real friend of yours, are they?

✔ **Messages identified as spam by another spam filter:** If your ISP or mail provider uses spam-filtering software, spam may arrive in your mailbox with `***SPAM***` or `Suspected Spam` on the Subject line. If you find that the spam filter reliably identifies messages as spam, you may as well create a filter that trashes those messages.

In many e-mail programs, filters are case sensitive — that is, capitalization counts. This feature (bug?) means that if you tell a filter to look for *Viagra,* it doesn't find messages that contain *viagra* instead. You may need to create multiple filters, one for each common capitalization. See the nearby sidebar, "Sneaky ways spammers evade filters," for more filtering tricks and traps.

Another Approach: Filter Everything Except Spam

Because identifying spam is hard when you're creating filters, you may want to do just the opposite: Identify the people you *do* want to hear from and move their messages into a folder of messages that you're sure you want to read. For example, you may create a bunch of filters like these:

✔ **Friends and family:** Create a folder named Friends And Family. Create for each of your friends and family members a filter that automatically moves messages from these folks into the folder. These messages are the ones that you're sure to want to read (depending on how well you get along with your family).

✔ **Work:** Create a folder named Coworkers or Colleagues. Create filters for the people you work with, to move their messages into this folder. If you work with several different groups of people (for example, paid work and volunteer work), create a separate folder for each group so that you can keep your projects straight.

✔ **Newsletters and mailing lists:** Create a folder for each discussion mailing list you participate in and a News folder for news. Make filters to move these messages into their appropriate folders.

Which E-Mail Program Do You Use?

Exactly how to create and use filters depends on which e-mail program you use. As spam becomes a larger issue, some programs have added rudimentary built-in spam filtering. Some have blocked sender lists, safe sender lists, and other types of filters.

Table 5-1 lists the programs we discuss and tells how to determine which one you're using and which chapter of this book describes its spam-fighting features.

Table 5-1	Some Popular E-Mail Programs	
Program	*What the Title Bar Says*	*Where It Comes From*
Outlook Express	Outlook Express	Windows itself (see Chapter 6).
Outlook	Microsoft Outlook	Microsoft Office. Outlook is similar to Outlook Express, but has more features (see Chapter 6).

(continued)

Table 5-1 *(continued)*

Program	What the Title Bar Says	Where It Comes From
Netscape Mail	Netscape	The Netscape browser. Earlier versions (Version 4.x) are rather different from later versions (Version 7.0 and later). If you have a version earlier than 7.0, go to www.netscape.com to download and install a new one (see Chapter 7).
Mozilla	Mozilla	The Mozilla browser, the open-source browser on which Netscape 7 is based (see Chapter 7).
Eudora	Eudora	www.eudora.com. Eudora is our favorite shareware e-mail program. The paid version has extra spam-filtering features (see Chapter 8).
Pegasus	Pegasus	www.pmail.com. Pegasus is our favorite free e-mail program (see Chapter 8).
AOL	America Online	www.aol.com or AOL CDs. AOL connects to the Internet and allows you to send Internet e-mail (see Chapter 9).
AOL	AOL Communicator	www.aol.com/downloads or AOL keyword **AOL Communicator** (see Chapter 9).
Hotmail	(Browser window)	www.hotmail.com, a Web site through which you can send and receive e-mail. Hotmail users can also read and send messages via Outlook Express (see Chapter 10).
Yahoo Mail!	(Browser window)	mail.yahoo.com, another Web-based e-mail service. If you pay $20 per year, you can use almost any e-mail program to send and receive your Yahoo Mail! messages (see Chapter 10).

If you use another e-mail program, don't despair — poke around your e-mail program to look for features that look like filters. Or, skip to Part III, which talks about spam-blocking programs regardless of which e-mail program you use.

Sneaky ways spammers evade filters

Spammers are smart — if they weren't, outraged Internet users would have shut them down long ago. Every time spam filterers come up with another way to spot spam, spammers change what they send out. It's like a sped-up version of e-mail evolution.

Here are some tricks that spammers use to prevent your filters from catching their junk messages:

✔ **Funky capitalization:** Most mail filter programs look for the exact capitalization you specify. If your filter looks for `spammersrus.com` on the From line, you don't catch messages from `Spammers Rus.com` or `spaMmersruS.com`.

✔ **No text:** Many spam messages contain almost no text, just a graphical image of text. By sending the text as a graphical image, filters can't read the text to spot the phrases you're looking for.

✔ **Wrods Speled w.r.0.n.g:** People are remarkably good at making sense of garbled text, so it's not hard to garble text enough to defeat filters and remain legible to people.

✔ **Hidden bogus codes:** E-mail messages can contain HTML formatting codes, which are enclosed in <angle brackets>. These formatting codes can create bold (with the <b> code) and italics (with <i>) text in your messages. However, lots of codes have no meaning in HTML, like <m> and <n>, so your e-mail program ignores them when displaying messages. However, if these meaningless codes are sprinkled in your messages, your filters are prevented from finding the words you have flagged. For example, a filter that's looking for `make money` doesn't match a message that contains `ma<m>ke mon<n>ey`.

Chapter 6

Filtering Spam in Outlook Express and Outlook

● ●

In This Chapter

▶ Making folders for spam and other kinds of messages

▶ Turning on the built-in Outlook spam-blocking

▶ Adding spammers to your Blocked Senders or Junk Senders list

▶ Blocking graphics files that spammers use to track whether you have read the message (Outlook 2002)

▶ Making rules that tell Outlook Express and Outlook what to do with your spam

▶ Throwing spam right into the trash or parking it in a folder for later review

● ●

*M*icrosoft has two major e-mail programs: Outlook Express and Outlook. They're similar, but not identical, and here's how you can tell which one you're using:

✔ **Outlook Express** (also called OE) comes free with Windows. We describe Outlook Express Version 6, which comes with Windows XP. You can also download Outlook Express 6 from the Internet Explorer Web site, at www. microsoft.com/ie. (Outlook Express comes with most downloadable versions of Internet Explorer too.) To run Outlook Express, choose Start➪Outlook Express, choose Start➪All Programs➪Outlook Express, or double-click the Outlook Express icon on your desktop.

✔ **Outlook** is part of the Microsoft Office suite of programs, which isn't downloadable — you have to buy it. We describe Outlook 2003 (which comes with Microsoft Office 2003), Outlook 2002 (which comes with Office XP), and Outlook 2000 (which comes with Office 2000). To run Outlook, choose Start⇨Microsoft Office Outlook, choose Start⇨Programs⇨Microsoft Office⇨Microsoft Office Outlook, or double-click the Outlook icon on your desktop.

This chapter describes how to set up the spam-filtering features of both programs, which include

- **Rules:** The Microsoft name for filters, rules can identify spam and send it to the trash.

- **Blocked Senders list:** If you get a message from anyone on this list, the message goes right into the trash. Outlook 2000 and 2002 call this feature the Junk Senders list.

- **Safe Senders list:** Messages from people on this list *don't* get marked as spam, even if the message looks like spam (Outlook 2003). Outlook 2000 and 2002 call it the Exception list.

- **Safe Recipients list:** Messages addressed to these mailing list addresses aren't marked as spam (Outlook 2003).

If you aren't familiar with how to send and receive e-mail, maintain an address book, attach files to messages, and perform other tasks in Outlook and Outlook Express, see *The Internet For Dummies,* by John R. Levine, Carol Baroudi, and Margaret Levine Young, some of the same lovable authors of this book (published by Wiley Publishing, Inc.).

Outlook Express can read and send Usenet newsgroup messages in addition to e-mail messages. (If you don't know what we're talking about, *Usenet* is an Internet-based worldwide system of discussion groups — see our Web page net.gurus. com/usenet for information about how to use it.) The Outlook Express spam-filtering features work for newsgroup messages too.

A number of third-party spam-filtering programs are specifically designed to work with Outlook and Outlook Express (see Chapter 11 for details).

Outlook and Outlook Express are renowned for having security holes that allow viruses, Trojan horse programs, and other nasty critters to hijack your computer and turn it into a spam machine. If you use either program, you need to keep on top of the latest security patches and *always* have a current, working, and regularly updated antivirus program installed on your computer. If you need tips and recommendations for avoiding viruses, pick up a copy of *Internet Privacy For Dummies* (also published by Wiley Publishing, Inc.).

Folders Are Your Friends

Outlook Express and Outlook come with a bunch of folders, including Inbox, Outgoing Mail (or Outbox), and Deleted Items. Recent versions of Outlook also have a Junk E-Mail or Junk Mail folder for use with its built-in spam-spotting features — you can use this folder for messages that you too identify as spam.

What folders do you have?

The list of folders usually appears down the left side of the program window, as shown in Figure 6-1. If you don't see it, choose View⇨Navigation Pane (in Outlook 2003), View⇨ Folder List (in Outlook 2000 and Outlook 2002), or View⇨ Layout and then select the Folder List check box (in Outlook Express).

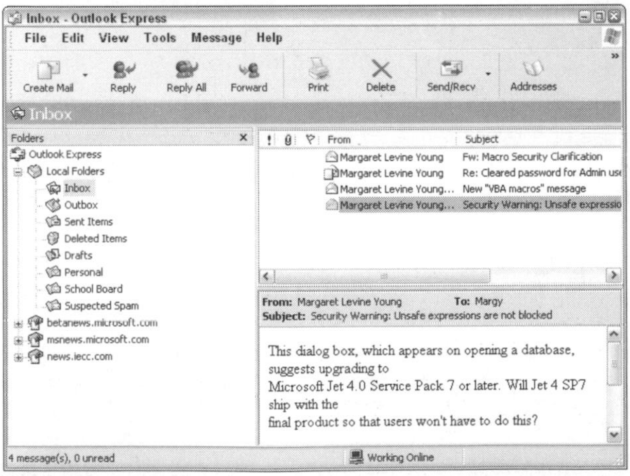

Figure 6-1: Outlook Express and Outlook list your mail folders down the left side. (We added the Suspected Spam folder.)

The general idea is to get spam out of your Inbox folder and into the Deleted Items, Junk E-Mail, or other folder so that you don't have to read it.

Creating a folder for your spam

If you want to create a folder named Suspected Spam into which you filter suspected spam messages, follow these steps:

1. **On the folder list, select the folder in which you want to store this new folder.**

   We usually select Local Folders, Personal Folders, or Outlook Today.

2. **Choose File➪New➪Folder from the menu bar. Or, right-click Local Folders or Personal Folders on the list of folders and choose New Folder from the menu that appears. Or, press Ctrl+Shift+E.**

   One way or the other, you see the Create Folder dialog box, as shown in Figure 6-2. Outlook shows the Create New Folder dialog box. It looks pretty much the same, but with an extra box in which you select what kind of items the folder holds; leave the box set to Mail And Post Items.

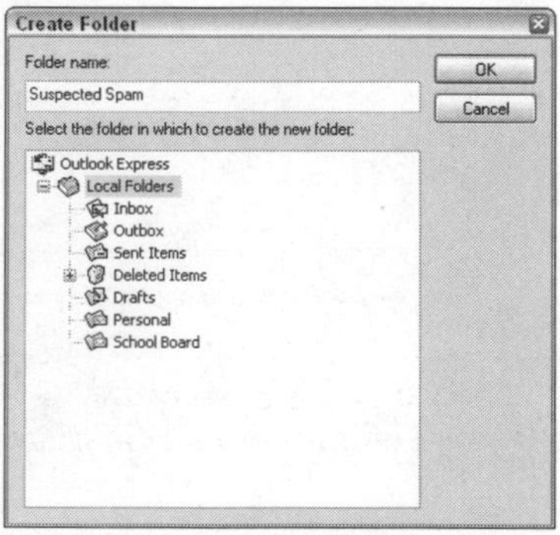

Figure 6-2: Create a folder for messages you identify as spam.

3. **In the Folder name box, type the name for your new folder.**

4. Select Local Folders or Personal Folders on the list of folders so that the new folder is contained in that folder.

5. Click OK.

Your new folder appears on the folder list. To see what's in it (nothing yet), double-click it. If you decide later to remove or rename it, right-click it and choose Delete or Rename from the menu that appears. You can also drag-and-drop folders to locations on your folder list, even inside other folders.

Turning On Junk E-Mail Blocking (Outlook 2003)

Outlook 2003 has a new spam-spotting feature that looks at each incoming message and assigns it a Spam Confidence Level (SCL) number. The SCL number is based on a bunch of factors that Microsoft is a little vague about. (See the sidebar "Bayesian what?" in Chapter 11 to find out how advanced filtering techniques work.)

We don't find that the SCL-based system Outlook 2003 uses catches much spam. But perhaps it will improve over time.

Spam-blocking levels in Outlook 2003

You never see the SCL number for each message, but you can tell Outlook 2003 to filter out messages based on their SCL levels. You can set Outlook 2003 to throw out messages based on each message's SCL, setting a high, medium, or low level depending on how nervous you are about nonspam messages getting inadvertently trashed.

To tell Outlook what to do with messages, you can set the Outlook junk e-mail blocking to one of four levels:

- ✔ **No Automatic Filtering:** Turns SCL-based blocking off. We recommend this level if you love reading spam or if you're using another program to spot spam (like one of the programs we describe in Chapter 11).

✓ **Low:** The default setting, which spots e-mail that has a moderate to high SCL number and moves it to your Junk E-Mail folder.

✓ **High:** Junks e-mail that has a low, medium, or high SCL number and may catch real messages too. Only messages with *very* low SCL numbers get through. Be sure to check the messages in your Junk E-Mail folder regularly if you use this setting, to check for *false positives* (good e-mail misidentified as spam).

✓ **Safe Lists Only:** Turns off SCL-based blocking. Junks all e-mail except messages from people on your Safe Senders list or Safe Recipients list. See the section "Letting Mail from Your Buddies Through" to find out how to add people to these lists.

Setting Outlook 2003 to block your spam

To set your junk e-mail blocking level, follow these steps:

1. **Choose Tools⇨Options from the menu.**

   You see the Options dialog box with the Preferences tab selected.

2. **On the Preferences tab, click the Junk E-Mail button.**

   You see the Junk E-Mail Options dialog box, as shown in Figure 6-3.

3. **Select the No Automatic Filtering, Low, High, or Safe Lists Only option to set your junk e-mail filtering level.**

4. **If you want your junk mail to be deleted completely rather than moved to the Junk E-Mail folder, select the check box at the bottom of the dialog box.**

   We don't recommend this setting if you're using the high level of spam-blocking.

5. **Click OK and then OK again to dismiss both dialog boxes.**

Figure 6-3: Turning on the Outlook 2003 spam-blocking feature.

An advantage to letting Outlook move spam to the Junk E-Mail folder rather than immediately delete it is that the Outlook SCL isn't perfect. (No spam-identification system is perfect!) From time to time, or if you were expecting a message that never came, you can look over the messages that Outlook thinks are spam by opening your Junk E-Mail folder. See the section "Reviewing Your Spam," later in this chapter, to find out how to look at and then empty this folder.

When Outlook 2003 spots an incoming piece of spam, you see the warning message shown in Figure 6-4.

Figure 6-4: Spam alert!

If you're just starting to use spam-blocking in Outlook 2003, we suggest that you let the program move suspected spam into the Junk E-Mail folder for several weeks and monitor what it moves. If you don't see any false positives after a couple of weeks, follow the steps in this section again and select the check box in Step 4.

Telling Outlook 2003 who your friends are

Outlook 2003 junk e-mail blocking may catch messages that you really want to read (called false positives). One way of overriding the program's SCL-based ranking system is to specify the addresses and domains of your buddies and work associates — or any address from which you never want messages to be considered as spam.

You can ensure that messages from your friends and coworkers don't get classified as spam, even if they *do* talk about mortgages, debt reduction, or the enlargement of various body parts, by adding them to your Safe Senders list. Here's how:

1. **Open a message from one of these people.**

2. **Choose Actions⇨Junk E-Mail⇨Add Sender to Safe Senders List.**

   You see a message confirming the addition.

3. **Click OK.**

You can see the Safe Senders list by choosing Tools⇨Options, clicking the Junk E-Mail button, and clicking the Safe Senders tab in the Junk E-Mail Options dialog box that appears. You can add the address of each of your buddies by clicking Add, typing the address, and clicking OK.

Outlook maintains a Contacts list (address book, actually), which you can see by choosing Go⇨Contacts or pressing Ctrl+3. (Choose Go⇨Mail or press Ctrl+1 to get back to your mail.) On the Safe Senders tab in the Junk E-Mail Options dialog box, a check box at the bottom of the dialog box tells Outlook to automatically treat all e-mail addresses on your Contacts list as safe senders. We recommend that you leave this check box selected.

Telling Outlook 2003 which mailing lists you're on

If you subscribe to mailing lists or e-mail newsletters, Outlook 2003 may decide that their messages are spam. Many newsletters use lots of graphics and sales talk and could easily earn a high SCL ranking. To prevent your mailing list and newsletter messages from disappearing in the Junk E-Mail folder, add their addresses to your Safe Recipients list.

Unlike the Safe Senders list, the Safe Recipients list looks at the address on the To line of incoming messages. When you get messages from a mailing list or e-mail newsletter, the address of the newsletter usually appears on the To line of the message. For example, if you subscribe to a mailing list that discusses raising chickens at home, messages may be addressed to hens-at-home@gurus.com. To tell Outlook 2003 that the current message from a mailing list isn't spam, choose Actions⇨Junk E-Mail⇨Add Recipient to Safe Recipients List. You can review the entries on the list by choosing Tools⇨ Options, clicking the Junk E-Mail button, and clicking the Safe Recipients tab.

Turning On Junk E-Mail Blocking (Outlook 2000 and Outlook 2002)

Neither Outlook 2000 nor Outlook 2002 has the more sophisticated Outlook 2003 ways of spotting spam; they identify spam only by the address of the sender or addressee or by words or phrases on the Subject line or in the text of a message. Although the following sections tell you how to tell Outlook the addresses of spam, first you need to turn this feature on.

To tell Outlook 2000 or Outlook 2002 to move messages to your Deleted Items folder based on the sender's address, follow these steps:

1. **Click to select Inbox on your folder list.**

2. **Click the Organize button on the toolbar.**

   The Ways To Organize Inbox pane appears in the upper-right part of the Outlook window.

3. **Click the Junk E-Mail link.**

   The pane shown in Figure 6-5 appears in the upper-right part of the Outlook window. The pane shows what Outlook plans to do with messages it identifies as junk. The default is to display these messages in gray.

Figure 6-5: Junking spam in Outlook 2000 or 2002.

4. **Click in the Color box and choose Move from the menu that appears.**

   The other box changes to show the name of the folder where Outlook moves spam: your Junk E-Mail folder.

5. **Click the Turn On button.**

   If you don't already have a Junk E-Mail folder, Outlook offers to make you one: Click OK and click the No button to avoid creating a shortcut to it. Now the message says New Junk messages will be moved to Junk E-Mail.

6. **Click the Organize button again to close the Ways To Organize Inbox pane.**

Fooling with Filters.txt (Outlook 2000 and Outlook 2002)

Outlook 2000 and 2002 come with a list of words and phrases that appear in spam, and where to look for them, in the form of a text file full of rules. Look for the file Filters.txt in your C:\Program Files\Microsoft Office\ Office or C:\Program Files\Microsoft Office\Office10\1033 folder. (If you can't find the file in those folders, search your hard disk for the file-name.). The rules in Filters.txt look like this:

From is blank
Subject contains "advertisement"
Body contains "money back"
Body contains "cards accepted"

You can also create your own rules to extend the spam-spotting abilities in Outlook, as explained in the section "Creating Rules to Trash Spam," later in this chapter.

See the section "Creating a new rule in Outlook 2000 or
Outlook 2002," at the end of this chapter, to find out how to
add the addresses of your friends to your Exception list so
that filters don't classify their messages as spam.

Blocking Messages by Sender

Both Outlook and Outlook Express can filter out messages
from specific addresses. To block messages from a specific
address, follow these steps:

1. **Open a message from the address.**

2. **In the window that displays the message, choose
   Message⇨Block Sender (in Outlook Express),
   Actions⇨Junk E-Mail⇨Add Sender To Blocked
   Senders List (in Outlook 2003), or Actions⇨Junk
   E-Mail⇨Add To Junk Senders list (in Outlook 2000
   and Outlook 2002).**

   You may see a message confirming that the address
   has been added to your Blocked Senders or Junk
   Senders list.

3. **If you see a confirmation message, click OK.**

   The message you opened is still in your inbox; the program will block *future* messages, but doesn't do anything about this one. Just delete it!

Viewing your Blocked Senders list

You can look at or edit the Blocked Senders list later, in case
you add a friend accidentally or you want to type a bunch of
spammer addresses. The commands are different for Outlook
Express and Outlook:

- ✔ **Outlook Express:** Choose Tools⇨Message Rules⇨
  Blocked Senders List from the menu bar in the main
  Outlook Express window. You see the Message Rules
  dialog box with the Blocked Senders tab selected, as
  shown in Figure 6-6.

- ✔ **Outlook 2003:** Choose Tools⇨Options and select the
  Junk E-Mail option on the Preferences tab. Click the
  Blocked Senders tab, which looks much like Figure 6-6.

✔ **Outlook 2000 and Outlook 2002:** Select Inbox on your folder list. Click the Organize button on the toolbar. The Ways To Organize Inbox pane appears in the upper-right part of the Outlook window. Click the <u>Junk E-Mail</u> link. Click the <u>Click Here</u> link that offers to show you options. Click the <u>Edit Junk Senders</u> link to display the small Edit Junk Senders dialog box.

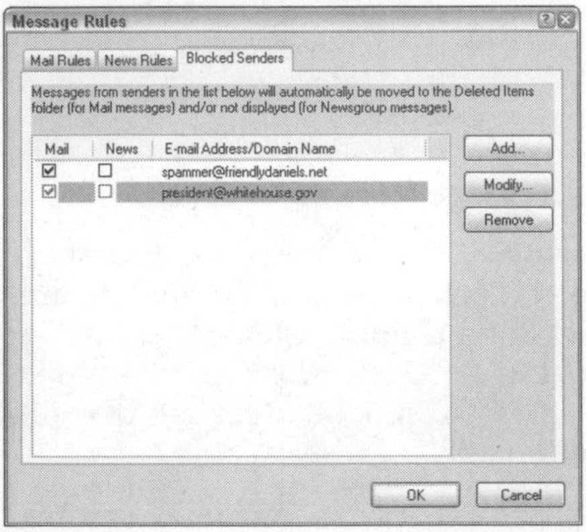

Figure 6-6: You can block all incoming messages from specific addresses.

Messages from any addresses on your Blocked Senders list are shunted straight to your Deleted Items or Junk E-Mail folder (unless you use Outlook 2003 and have selected the check box to delete these messages immediately, as described in the preceding section).

You can add more addresses by clicking Add and typing or pasting the address in the dialog box that appears. If you decide to accept messages from an address after all, you can delete it from the list by choosing the address and clicking Remove. To edit an entry on the list, select it and click either the Modify or Edit button.

Blocking messages from entire domains

The Blocked Senders list can include entire domains (a *domain* is the part of an e-mail address after the @). For example, if you don't want to receive *any* mail from the White House,

you could block all messages that come from *anything@*
whitehouse.gov. Follow these steps to block all messages
from an entire domain:

1. **Display the Blocked Senders list, as described in the
   preceding section.**

2. **Click the Add button.**

   Outlook Express displays the Add Sender dialog box,
   as shown in Figure 6-7. Outlook shows a smaller dialog
   box, but you get the idea.

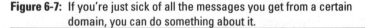

Figure 6-7: If you're just sick of all the messages you get from a certain
domain, you can do something about it.

3. **Type the domain name and click OK.**

   In Outlook Express, leave the Mail Messages radio
   button selected. When you click OK, the new entry
   appears on your Blocked Senders list. An at-sign (@)
   may appear at the beginning of the entry; that's okay.

Reviewing Your Spam

If you have just set up or updated spam-blocking features or
mail-filtering rules (described later in this chapter), be sure to
look through the messages that Outlook Express or Outlook
has identified as spam. You can easily create a rule that is
too broad and creates false positives — perfectly innocent
messages that may have been mislabeled as spam.

To look in your Deleted Items, Junk E-Mail, Suspected Spam,
or whatever folder you shunt spam into, double-click it on the
folder list. The list of messages in that folder appears. Scroll
through the messages; the unread messages appear in bold.
(Spam you never saw should all appear in bold.)

If you see any good messages, drag them into your Inbox folder. Then look at the message and at your message rules to figure out how it got tagged as spam, and fix your rules.

If you're looking at your Junk E-Mail folder in Outlook 2003, Outlook may have assigned the wrong SCL level to a message, causing it to end up in with the spam. You can tell Outlook that it guessed wrong about this message being spam. Follow these steps:

1. **With the message selected or open, choose Actions⇨ Junk E-Mail⇨Mark As Not Junk (or press Ctrl+Alt+J).**

   You see the Mark As Not Junk dialog box, as shown in Figure 6-8.

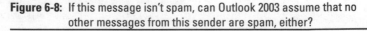

Figure 6-8: If this message isn't spam, can Outlook 2003 assume that no other messages from this sender are spam, either?

2. **If messages from this sender should never be considered spam, leave the top check box selected.**

   For example, if the message was from `president@ whitehouse.gov`, you may want to leave the check box selected so that you can always read these messages. Or, depending on your politics, you may want all messages from this address to be deep-sixed — in that case, deselect the top check box (so that it doesn't contain a check).

   If this check box contains a check mark, Outlook adds this address to your Safe Senders list.

3. **If the message was addressed to a mailing list address (if a mailing list address, rather than your own e-mail address, appears on the To line), select the check box for the mailing list address in the Always Trust E-Mail Sent To The Following Addresses list.**

   If the message was sent to several addresses, each address appears on the list with its own check box. If a check box on this list contains a check mark, Outlook adds the address to your Safe Recipients list.

4. **Click OK.**

   Outlook adds the addresses to the appropriate lists.

Blocking Web Bugs Disguised as Graphics (Outlook 2003)

Originally, e-mail contained only boring, unformatted text, but those days are long gone. Lots of e-mail messages contain graphic files, both to add pictures to the messages and to provide formatting elements, like logos, headlines, and borders.

However, graphics in e-mail messages have a dark side. Spammers sometimes include specially coded links to pictures that are stored in files back on their file servers. When you open the message, your e-mail program fetches the picture to display by using the special code linked to your e-mail address and — voila! — the spammer knows that you have read the message and that your address is good. The result? You get lots more spam. This type of trick graphic is sometimes called a *Web bug*.

Outlook 2003 turns off the automatic display of all pictures in e-mail messages to prevent just this kind of tracking, using its Automatic Picture Blocking feature. Neither Outlook Express nor earlier versions of Outlook include picture blocking (and neither do most other e-mail programs). If you don't have Outlook 2003, you still may want to read it to understand how it works.

How Outlook 2003 displays pictures

With automatic picture blocking turned on (the default setting), pictures in e-mail messages appear as little red Xs. A message at the top also lets you know that pictures weren't downloaded. Figure 6-9 shows a message with its pictures surgically removed.

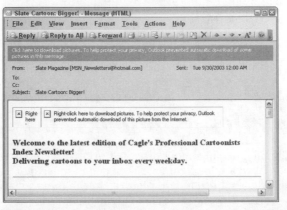

Figure 6-9: Instructions at the top of this message window tell you how to download pictures that Outlook 2003 has blocked.

If you want to see the pictures in the message, click the pictures-missing notice at the top of the message. Or, right-click a red X in the message. Then choose Download Pictures from the menu that appears. Outlook displays the graphics that were missing.

Luckily, you can tell Outlook to download the pictures in messages from folks you trust. If a message with an attached picture arrives from someone on your Safe Senders or Safe Recipients list, Outlook downloads the pictures anyway. Outlook figures that because you know these folks, pictures from them are safe. Just add addresses to your Safe Senders list (for individuals) or Safe Recipients list (for newsletters and mailing lists whose messages arrive addressed to the list address rather than to you). When the message is open, click in the pictures-missing message and select Add Sender To Safe Senders List.

Turning off the Outlook 2003 picture-blocking feature

If you would rather bag the whole picture-blocking feature and not worry about Web bugs, you can. Follow these steps:

1. **Choose Tools⇨Options in the main Outlook window.**

   You see the Options dialog box.

2. **Click to select the Security tab.**

3. **Click the Change Automatic Download Settings button.**

   You see the Automatic Picture Download Settings dialog box, as shown in Figure 6-10. Normally, all four check boxes are selected.

Figure 6-10: Turning off automatic picture blocking in Outlook 2003.

4. **If you want Outlook 2003 to download all pictures automatically, click to deselect the first check box.**

   This action may allow spammers to track you, but it also allows you to get nicely formatted messages from people who aren't on your Contacts list or Safe Senders list. We recommend leaving this check box selected, but it's up to you.

5. **If you don't even want Outlook to download pictures from people on your Safe Senders, Safe Recipients, or Contacts lists, clear the second check box.**

   This choice looks a little paranoid to us, frankly.

6. **If you have set up security zones in Internet Explorer and you don't even want Outlook to download pictures from sites in your trusted zone, clear the third check box.**

   No one we know has ever bothered to configure a Trusted Zone list, which is part of Internet Explorer. To take a look at it, switch to Internet Explorer, choose Tools⇨Options, select the Security tab, click the Trusted Sites icon, and click the Sites button. If you see sites you don't trust, select them and click the Remove button. (We found that free.aol.com had added itself to our list, and we removed it immediately.)

7. **If you don't want Outlook to bother warning you when you're working with messages that contain attachments, select the fourth check box.**

   We recommend leaving this check box selected.

8. **Click OK and then click OK again to make all those dialog boxes go away.**

Sorting Spam Directly into the Trash

You can create rules that tell Outlook Express or Outlook to sort some messages directly into the Delete Items, Junk E-Mail, or other folder. Some of the third-party spam-filtering programs described in Chapter 11 add tags to incoming messages to indicate that the messages are probably spam. You can create rules to sort these tagged messages in the Junk E-Mail, Deleted Items, or other folder.

First, create a folder if you don't already have one for spam, as described in the section "Creating a Folder for Your Spam," earlier in this chapter. Then you're ready to create spam filters!

If you use Outlook 2003, you may as well use the Junk E-Mail folder that you already have — there's no need to create a new folder.

Creating Rules to Trash Spam

You can create a bunch of *rules* that tell Outlook Express or Outlook what a particular spam message looks like and what to do with it — mainly, to get it the heck out of your inbox! The e-mail program applies each rule to each message as it arrives in your inbox; and, by creating rules that match the headers or text of spam messages, you can deflect spam from your inbox into another folder.

 If you use any of the Outlook junk e-mail filtering features, Outlook tries to spot spam and move it into the Junk E-Mail folder. Outlook may miss much of it, though. Rules allow you to specify additional spam to move.

 Rules don't work with Web-based mailboxes, like Hotmail. Rules don't work with IMAP-based mailboxes either (these mailboxes, used mainly in large organizations, allow you to read mail on the mail server without downloading it for storage on your computer).

You can make pretty fancy rules. For example, you can specify that if a message contains the phrase *low interest mortgage* or *debt reduction* and it's *not* from your bank, it should be deleted. You can make lots of rules, one for each type of spam you get. The more you make, the more spam never hits your inbox.

 See the section in Chapter 5 about identifying spam for filtering for suggestions about how to specify which messages are spam.

Creating a new rule in Outlook Express

To work with rules, choose Tools⇨Message Rules⇨Mail to display the Message Rules dialog box, as shown in Figure 6-11. If you haven't created any rules yet, Outlook Express displays the New Mail Rule dialog box, as shown in Figure 6-12. From the Message Rules dialog box, click the New button to create a new rule.

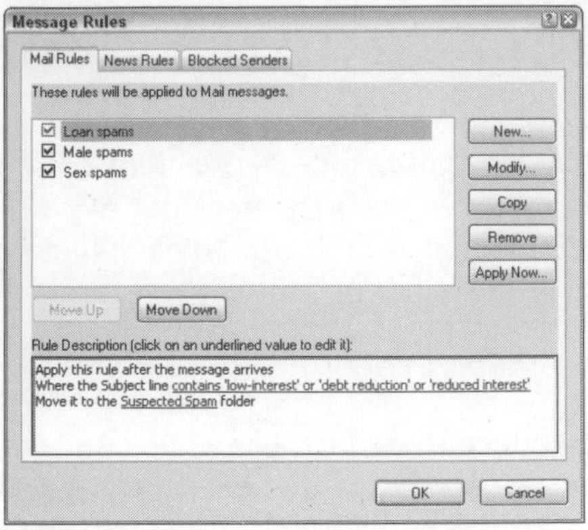

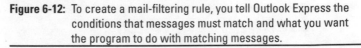

Figure 6-11: You can create, modify, and delete mail-filtering rules in Outlook Express.

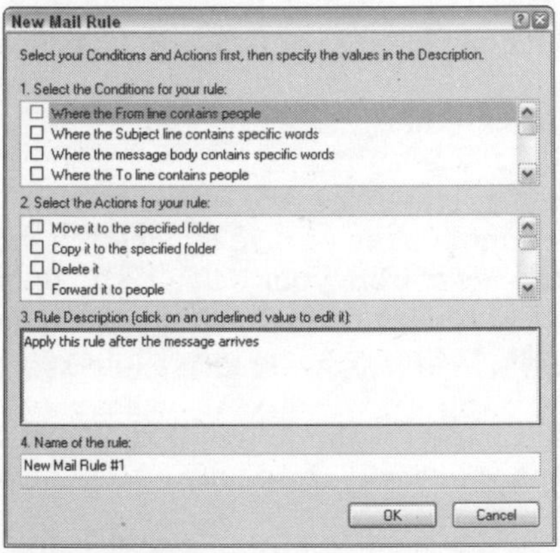

Figure 6-12: To create a mail-filtering rule, you tell Outlook Express the conditions that messages must match and what you want the program to do with matching messages.

The New Mail Rule dialog box contains four boxes in which you specify information about the rule:

> ✔ **Select The Conditions For Your Rule:** You specify which parts of the message Outlook Express should look at in determining to which messages to apply the rule. You can select the From line, Subject line, message body, To line, CC line, priority, mail account, size, attachment, and security setting. Or, you can choose to apply the rule to

all messages. Strangely, you don't specify the text, address, or other information here; you provide this information in Box 3. Go figure.

✔ **Select The Actions For Your Rule:** You specify what Outlook Express should do when a message matches a condition. You can move a message to a folder, copy it to a folder, delete it, forward it, reply to it, or mark it as highlighted, flagged, read, or unread. You can also tell Outlook Express not to download the message from your mail server or to delete it from the mail server without downloading it.

✔ **Rule Description:** This box shows the rule as you create it. You specify details about the rule, such as what text to look for or which folder to move messages to, by clicking underlined links in the description.

✔ **Name Of The Rule:** You can name the rule. (If you don't, Outlook Express comes up with creative names, like New Mail Rule #1.)

Follow these steps to create a rule to filter out spam:

1. **In Box 1, Select The Conditions For Your Rule, select the check box for the part of the message that identifies the message as spam.**

   For example, if you want to block all messages that contain the phrase *low interest mortgage* on the Subject line, select the second check box, Where The Subject Line Contains Specific Words.

2. **In Box 2, Select The Actions For Your Rule, select the first check box, Move It To The Specified Folder.**

   Box 3 now shows text based on your choice in Boxes 1 and 2. For example, if you selected the Subject Line check box in Box 1, Box 3 says

   ```
   Apply this rule after this message arrives.
   When the Subject line contains specific
   words, move it to the specified folder.
   ```

3. **In Box 3, Rule Description, click the <u>Contains Specified Words</u> link to specify the word or phrase to match.**

   You see the Type Specific Words dialog box, as shown in Figure 6-13.

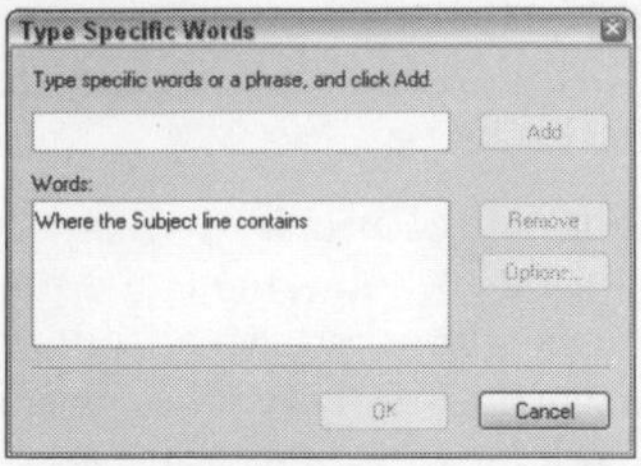

Figure 6-13: Which word or phrase appears in spam?

4. **Type the word or phrase that appears in the spam you want to trash. Click the Add button.**

   For example, type **low-interest** in the box. When you click the Add button, the Words box shows the words you're looking for.

5. **If you want the rule to look for another phrase too, repeat Step 4.**

   You may want the same rule to look for other loan and mortgage spam messages, so you can type **debt reduction** and click the Add button and then type **reduced interest** and click Add again. The Words box shows the whole list of words and phrases you want the rule to match.

6. **Click OK to return to the New Mail Rule dialog box.**

   Box 3 shows the list of phrases the rule matches. But you still haven't told the rule what to do with messages that contain these phrases on the Subject line.

7. **Click the <u>Specified</u> link in Box 3.**

   Outlook Express displays the Move dialog box, showing a list of your folders (as shown in Figure 6-14).

8. **Select the folder and click OK.**

   We like to move spam to a Suspected Spam folder, which we look through from time to time, to check for good messages that may have been misidentified as spam. Your other option is to move the messages directly into the Deleted Items folder.

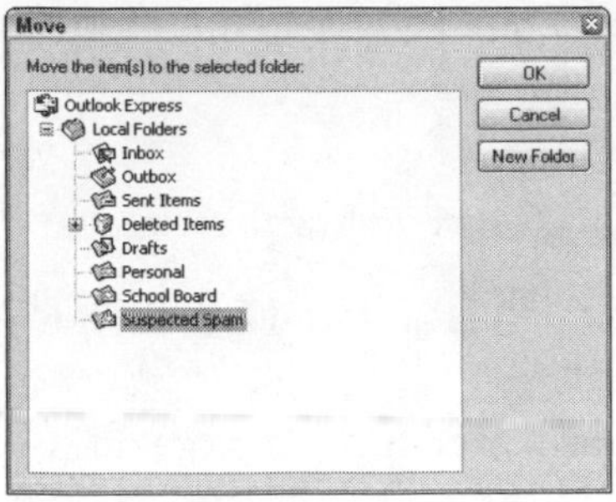

Figure 6-14: Where do you want to put your spam?

9. **Click to select the Stop Processing More Rules check box in Box 2 (Select The Actions For Your Rule).**

   The phrase *and stop processing more rules* appears at the end of your rules description, telling Outlook Express that, after it has moved a message once, it's done applying rules to that message; it's time to go on to the next message.

10. **In Box 4, Name Of The Rule, type a name for this rule.**

    You can use any name; you're the only person who sees it. Type something that makes finding the rule easy if you decide to change it later, such as **loan spams**.

11. **Click OK.**

    Outlook Express stores the rule and you return to the Message Rules dialog box.

 Some spam-tagging programs (like POPFile, which is described in Chapter 11) add a header to each message that indicates whether the message is spam. POPFile can add a header line that says `X-Text-Classification: spam` to suspected spam messages. However, Outlook Express can't filter messages based on the X-Text-Classification header. Instead, you need to tell POPFile (or whatever spam filter you use) to use Subject-line tagging, and apply filters based on the `[spam]` tag or other tag added to the Subject lines of suspected junk messages.

Creating a new rule in Outlook 2003

To work with rules in Outlook, follow these steps:

1. **Choose Tools⇨Rules and Alerts from the main Outlook window.**

   If you have Outlook configured to get messages from a Hotmail account, you see a message warning you that rules don't work with Hotmail; just click OK.

   The Rules and Alerts dialog box opens.

2. **If the Manage Alerts tab is selected, click to select the E-Mail Rules tab.**

   You see the dialog box shown in Figure 6-15.

3. **If you use Outlook to check more than one mail account, set the Apply Changes To This Folder box to the Inbox folder of the account to which you want these rules to apply.**

Figure 6-15: Outlook 2003 lets you set up lots of rules to spot spam.

If you set up rules in a previous version of Outlook, you can import them into Outlook 2003 by clicking the Options button on the E-Mail Rules tab and then clicking the Import Rules button.

To create a new rule, click the New Rule button (logically enough!). You see the Rules Wizard dialog box, as shown in Figure 6-16. The exact steps depend on whether you want to identify some spam messages by the From or To address or by words on the Subject line.

Figure 6-16: Outlook 2003 has templates and a wizard to help you create rules to separate spam from real messages.

 In the Rules Wizard dialog box, leave the Start Creating A Rule From A Template option selected. For sorting spam, one of the templates usually fits the bill.

Trapping spam based on the From or To address (Outlook 2003)

Follow these steps to create a new rule to identify spam by its To or From address:

1. **In the Stay Organized section of the Step 1 box, click to select the option Move Messages From Someone To A Folder to match spam from a specific address. Or, select Move Messages Sent To A Distribution List To A Folder to match spam that comes with a bogus address on the To line.**

   The Step 2 box now contains text based on your choice. If you selected Move Messages From Someone To A Folder, the Step 2 box says

```
Apply this rule after the message arrives /
from people or distribution list / move it
to the specified folder
```

(Okay, so punctuation isn't Microsoft's long suit.) If you selected Move Messages Sent To A Distribution List To A Folder, it shows more or less the same message.

2. **Click the People Or Distribution List link in the Step 2 box.**

You see the Rule Address dialog box (see Figure 6-17).

Figure 6-17: Outlook 2003 wants to know the address of a spammer.

3. **Type the address in the From box near the bottom of the dialog box and click OK.**

If you selected Move Messages From Someone To A Folder in the Step 1 box, Outlook looks for these addresses on the From line of incoming messages. If you selected Move Messages Sent To A Distribution List To A Folder in the Step 1 box, Outlook looks at the To line.

When you click OK, you return to the Rules Wizard dialog box and the People Or Distribution List link is replaced with the address you typed.

4. **Click the Specified link in the Step 2 box, select the Junk E-Mail folder, and click OK.**

If you have created another folder to hold suspected spam, select that folder instead.

5. Click the Finish button.

The rule appears in the Rules and Alerts dialog box — it's ready to intercept spam!

 If you want the opportunity to tweak the settings for your rule, click the Next button rather than Finish in Step 5. The Rules Wizard shows you a series of dialog boxes in which you can specify the details of the rule, as shown in Figure 6-18. You can leave these settings alone, or you can scroll down the list of options and make changes.

Rules Wizard

Which condition(s) do you want to check?
Step 1: Select condition(s)

☑ on this machine only
☑ from people or distribution list
☐ with specific words in the subject
☐ through the specified account
☐ sent only to me
☐ where my name is in the To box
☐ marked as importance
☐ marked as sensitivity
☐ flagged for action
☐ where my name is in the Cc box
☐ where my name is in the To or Cc box
☐ where my name is not in the To box
☐ sent to people or distribution list

Step 2: Edit the rule description (click an underlined value)

Apply this rule after the message arrives
from friend@spammers.org
and on this machine only
move it to the Junk E-mail folder

Cancel | < Back | Next > | Finish

Figure 6-18: Tweaking the Rules Wizard settings.

Trapping spam based on words on the Subject line or in the body of the message (Outlook 2003)

Follow these steps to create a new rule to identify spam by its subject or text:

1. In the Stay Organized section of the Step 1 box, select the option Move Messages With Specific Words In The Subject To A Folder.

The Step 2 box now contains text based on your choice:

```
Apply this rule after the message arrives

with specific words in the subject

move it to the specified folder
```

2. **Click the <u>Specific Words</u> link in the Step 2 box.**

   You see the Search Text dialog box, as shown in Figure 6-19.

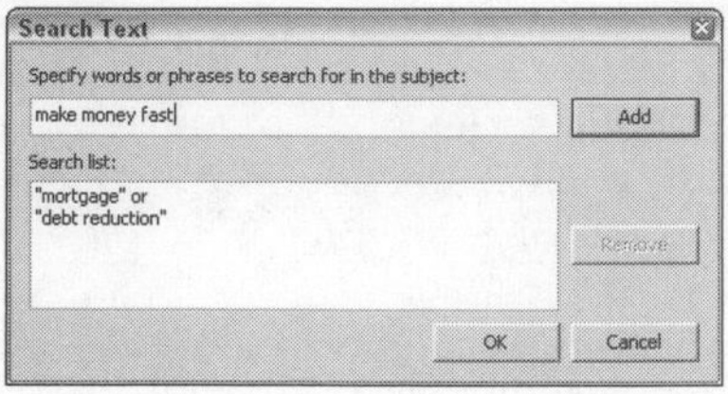

Figure 6-19: Typing typical spam phrases in Outlook 2003.

3. **In the top box in the Search Text dialog box, type a word or phrase that appears on the Subject line of spam and click the Add button.**

   Type words that appear *only* in spam, because Outlook moves all messages with these words out of your Inbox.

4. **Keeping typing words or phrases and clicking the Add button until you have entered a list of text that appears only in spam.**

5. **Click OK.**

   When you click OK, you return to the Rules Wizard dialog box and the <u>Specific Words</u> link is replaced with a list of the terms you typed.

6. **Click the <u>Specified</u> link in the Step 2 box, select the Junk E-Mail folder, and click OK.**

   If you have created another folder to hold suspected spam, select that folder instead.

7. **Click the Next button.**

   The wizard displays a list of conditions that it plans to use to determine which messages match the rule. The first item, With <u>Specific Words</u> In The Subject, is selected.

8. **If you want the rule to look in the body of messages for these words also, scroll down the list of conditions in the Step 1 box and select the With <u>Specific Words</u> In The Subject Or Body option so that a check mark appears in the box.**

Chances are, if a word or phrase identifies spam on the Subject line of messages, you don't want to read messages with those terms in the body of the message either.

9. **Click Finish.**

The rule appears in the Rules and Alerts dialog box.

Trapping spam based on the X-Text-Classification or other spam-tagging header

Some third-party spam programs examine your messages before they get to your e-mail program, adding a special header line indicating that the message is probably spam. (See Chapter 11 to find out how this process works.) For example, POPFile adds a header line with the text X-Text-Classification followed by a colon, a space, and the name of the bucket you created for spam.

Outlook 2003 can filter messages based on this header. Create a new rule and select Start From A Blank Rule rather than use a template. Click the Next button to see the box labeled Which Conditions Do You Want To Check. Select the With Specific Words In The Message Header link and then select the Specific Words link in the Step 2 box. Type **X-Text-Classification: spam** (or whatever the name of your suspected spam bucket is) as the text to match.

Fooling with Outlook 2003 rules

On the E-Mail Rules tab of the Rules and Alerts dialog box, you can tell Outlook to run all your rules right away — that is, apply all the rules against the messages that are already in your Inbox. Click the Run Rules Now button.

You can also edit existing rules by selecting the rule and clicking the Change Rule button, or delete rules by clicking the Delete button.

Creating a new rule in Outlook 2000 or Outlook 2002

Rules in Outlook 2000 and Outlook 2002 appear when you choose Tools⇨Rules Wizard from the menu. The Rules Wizard dialog box appears with a list of your mail-sorting rules, and two rules are already in place:

✔ **Junk E-Mail Rule:** This rule moves mail from people on your Junk Senders list to your Junk E-Mail list. (If this rule doesn't appear, refer to the section "Turning On Junk E-Mail Blocking (Outlook 2000 and Outlook 2002)," earlier in this chapter, to create it.)

✔ **Exception List:** This rule tells Outlook not to use the Junk E-Mail Rule on messages from your friends — that is, people whose addresses appear on your Exception list.

You have no need to create rules to identify spam by the address of the sender: Just add the addresses to your Junk Senders list, as described in the section "Blocking Messages by Sender," earlier in this chapter. But rules can be handy for identifying spam by words or phrases on the Subject line or in the text of the message.

Making a new rule (Outlook 2000 and Outlook 2002)

Follow these steps to create a rule to filter out spam:

1. **Choose Tools⇨Rules Wizard from the menu.**

   You see the Rules Wizard dialog box.

2. **Click the New button.**

   The Rules Wizard has a list of things you can do to a message.

3. **Select the option Move Messages Based On Content.**

   The Rules description box changes to read:

   Apply this rule after the message arrives with <u>specific words</u> in the subject or body move it to the specified folder

4. **Click the <u>Specific Words</u> link.**

   The Search Text dialog box appears (refer to Figure 6-19 in the preceding section).

5. **In the top box in the Search Text dialog box, type a word or phrase that appears on the Subject line or in the body of spam messages and click the Add button.**

   Type words that appear *only* in spam, because Outlook moves all messages with these words out of your Inbox.

6. **Keeping typing words or phrases and clicking the Add button until you have entered a list of text that appears only in spam.**

7. **Click OK.**

   When you click OK, you return to the Rules Wizard dialog box and the Specific Words link is replaced with a list of the terms you typed.

8. **Click the Specified link in the Rule description box, select the Junk E-Mail folder, and click OK.**

   If you have created another folder to hold suspected spam, select that folder instead.

9. **Click Finish.**

   The new rule appears in the Rule Wizard dialog box.

If you want to customize your rule, select it and click the Modify button. (You can't modify the Junk E-Mail or Exception List rules that Outlook created.) Rather than click Finish when you're done, you can click the Next button to see other options.

 To run your rules against the messages in your Inbox (or other folder), click the Run Now button, select the rule or rules to apply, select the folder, and click the Run Now button.

Whitelisting your friends (Outlook 2000 and Outlook 2002)

When you start filtering your messages, you need to make sure that messages from your buddies don't get caught by your spam-filtering rules. You can make a rule that Outlook applies first, telling it that if the sender is in your address book, not to apply any more rules to the message. Follow these steps:

1. **Choose Tools⇨Rules Wizard and click the New button to start a new rule.**

2. **Select the options Start From A Blank Rule and Check Messages When They Arrive and then click the Next button.**

3. **Select Where Sender Is In A Specified Address Book or From People Or Distribution List on the list on the next page of the wizard so that a check mark appears in its check box.**

4. **Click the <u>A Specified Address Book</u> or <u>People Or Distribution List</u> link and specify your buddies. Click the Next button.**

   In Outlook 2002, you select an entire address book. In Outlook 2000, you select individuals from your address book.

5. **Select the option Stop Processing More Rules on the list on the next page of the wizard so that a check mark appears in its check box.**

   This action tells Outlook not to apply the spam-filtering rules to these messages.

6. **Click the Finish button.**

   You may see a message telling you that the rule is processed only when Outlook is running; if so, click OK.

7. **In the Rules Wizard box, make sure that this rule appears first: if not, select it and click the Move Up button.**

   This rule needs to happen first, before Outlook gets around to applying the other rules.

Chapter 7

Filtering Spam in Netscape and Mozilla Mail

. . . .

In This Chapter

▶ Turning on the Netscape and Mozilla Mail built-in junk mail controls

▶ Creating folders for your spam

▶ Creating message filters that move spam directly into the trash

. . . .

*N*etscape was one of the earliest Web browsers, and for years it has come bundled with a respectable e-mail program, Netscape Mail. Versions of Netscape Mail up to 7.0 don't have strong anti-spam features, although they do enable you to create filters so that you can do some spam filtering on your own.

However, here's great news: Netscape Mail 7.1 added a powerful Bayesian anti-spam system that makes third-party spam filters unnecessary. If you use Netscape Mail 7.1, you can eliminate lots of spam by just turning on its spam feature.

This chapter describes Netscape 7.1, which you can download for free from browsers.netscape.com. An open source (non-commercial) version named Mozilla is also available (at www.mozilla.org), and this chapter describes Version 1.5. Because the two programs are so similar, we refer to them both as Netscape/Mozilla Mail.

If you have an earlier version of either program, upgrade right away so that you can take advantage of the new spam filters.

The main Netscape Mail window is shown in Figure 7-1. If you aren't familiar with how to send and receive e-mail with Netscape and Mozilla, see *The Internet For Dummies*, 9th Edition (written by John R. Levine, Margaret Levine Young, and Carol Baroudi and published by Wiley Publishing, Inc.). To open Netscape or Mozilla Mail from the Netscape or Mozilla browser window, choose Window⇨Mail & Newsgroups from the browser's menu bar.

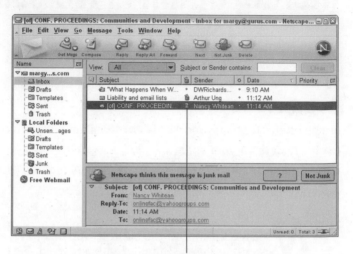

Junk Mail icon

Figure 7-1: Netscape 7 includes a browser and a mail program that has spam filtering built right in.

Netscape/Mozilla Mail has several privacy-related settings and features you can use to keep Netscape from coughing up your e-mail address to unknown Web sites and potential spammers. Instructions for using those features are in *Internet Privacy For Dummies* (written by John R. Levine, Ray Everett-Church, Greg Stebben, and David Lawrence and published by Wiley Publishing, Inc.).

Using the Netscape/Mozilla Mail Junk Mail Controls

Netscape/Mozilla Mail comes with built-in spam filtering. The program uses advanced Bayesian filtering, as described in Chapter 1. You don't need to install any of the third-party programs listed in Chapter 11 — the features of those programs are already built right in!

Configuring your junk mail controls

By default, the Junk Mail Controls feature is turned on, although you can turn it off or reconfigure it. Follow these steps:

1. **Click to select your e-mail account on the folder list on the left side of the Netscape/Mozilla Mail window.**

   If you have only one e-mail account (you poor, deprived soul!), it appears at the top of the list. If you have several accounts, you can set the junk mail controls separately for each account.

2. **Choose Tools⇨Junk Mail Controls from the Netscape/Mozilla Mail menu bar.**

   If you see an informational message, click OK. You see the Junk Mail Controls dialog box, as shown in Figure 7-2. The drop-down menu at the top shows which e-mail account you picked, if you have more than one.

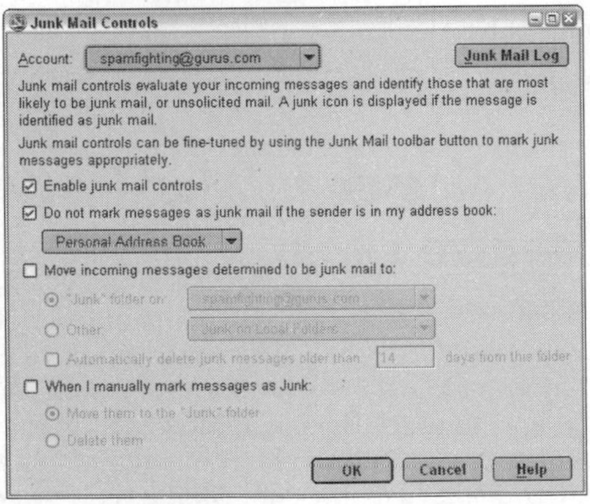

Figure 7-2: Netscape and Mozilla have built-in advanced Bayesian spam filtering!

3. **If the Enable Junk Mail Controls check box isn't selected, click it.**

   This step turns the junk mail controls on. Leave selected the check box that tells the program not to mark messages as spam if they come from people in your address book: Friends don't let friends send spam.

4. **Click the check box labeled Move Incoming Message Determined To Be Junk Mail To so that it contains a check mark.**

   Otherwise, the program marks messages with a little Junk Mail icon, and they still clutter your inbox.

5. **With the Junk Folder On option selected, set its drop-down menu to Local Folders.**

   The program moves your suspected spam to the Junk folder in the Local Folders section of the folder list.

6. **Click the When I Manually Mark Messages As Junk check box so that it contains a check mark, and then select whether to move them to the Junk or Trash folder.**

   If you have already determined that messages are spam, we figure "Why save them?" You may as well move them right to your Trash folder.

7. **Click OK.**

Training Netscape/Mozilla Mail to recognize spam

After you have configured your junk mail controls, Netscape/Mozilla Mail is ready to trash your spam. You have only one problem: It doesn't know how to tell spam from good mail. Your next step is to teach Netscape/Mozilla Mail to recognize spam when it sees it. If the program thinks that a message is spam, it either displays a little Junk Mail icon between the subject and the sender's name on the message list or moves the message to your Junk folder, depending on how you configured the program. Until you provide the program with some guidance, however, it's usually wrong.

To start training Netscape/Mozilla Mail to recognize spam, follow these steps:

- ✔ If a message is marked as junk mail or is in your Junk folder and it's *not* spam, display the message and click the Not Junk button.

- ✔ If a message is *not* marked as spam and it should be, click the little diamond between the subject and the sender's name so that the diamond turns into a Junk Mail icon.

As Netscape/Mozilla Mail repeatedly sees which messages you consider junk mail, it builds a list of words that usually appear in spam but not in other messages, and its guesses get better and better.

After marking spam and unmarking nonspam, you can delete all your junk mail messages by choosing Tools⇨Delete Mail Marked As Junk In Folder.

Creating a Folder for Your Spam (Or Other Messages)

Netscape/Mozilla Mail comes with a bunch of folders, such as Inbox, Drafts, Templates, Junk, Sent, and Trash. The folders stored on your own computer are listed under the Local Folders heading on the folder list on the left side of the Netscape/Mozilla Mail window (refer to Figure 7-1).

You don't need to create a folder for spam because Netscape/Mozilla Mail already comes with a Junk folder. However, if you want to make your own folder for spam you catch by using your own message filters (as described in the next section), follow these steps:

1. **Choose File⇨New⇨Folder.**

   You see the New Folder dialog box, as shown in Figure 7-3.

2. **Type a name for the folder in the Name box.**

   For example, you can make a folder named Personal for correspondence with your long-lost half-sister.

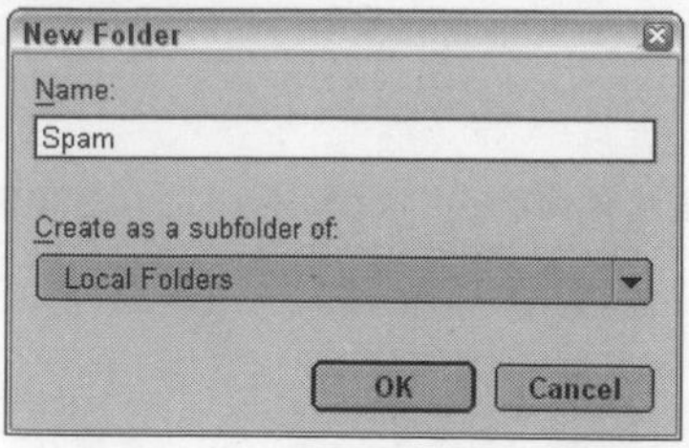

Figure 7-3: Creating folders in Netscape or Mozilla Mail.

3. **Click the dark drop-down list button and select Local Folders, and then pick the option Choose This One For The Parent from the menu that appears.**

   No, you're not creating a folder for messages from your parents. Folders can contain folders, and the program wants to know in which folder (the *parent* folder) to create your new folder. We think that this menu pick could be rewritten, maybe to say Main Folder or something similar.

4. **Click OK.**

   The folder appears in your Local Folders listing.

Creating Message Filters to Trash Spam

The Netscape/Mozilla Mail *message filters* tell the program what to do when it sees messages that match your specification. For example, you can move all messages from news@nytimes.com (the daily *New York Times*) to a News folder. Message filters are created and stored separately for each mail account you have, in case you retrieve messages from more than one e-mail account.

To create a message filter, follow these steps:

1. **Choose Tools⇨Message Filters.**

   You see the Message Filters dialog box, as shown in Figure 7-4.

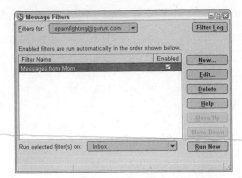

Figure 7-4: Message filters tell Netscape/Mozilla Mail what to do when it sees specific types of messages.

2. **If you have more than one e-mail account, set the Filters For drop-down list to the account you want to filter.**

3. **Click the New button.**

   You see the enormous Filter Rules dialog box, as shown in Figure 7-5.

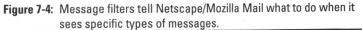

Figure 7-5: What messages does this rule work with, and what does it do?

4. **In the Filter name box, type a name for the filter.**

   The exact name doesn't matter: it's only for your use.

   The middle part of the window lists the criteria that identify the messages you want to do something to. You start with one criterion that says Subject and Contains.

   Figure 7-5 shows the window after you have created a rule. Before you do so, the buttons are labeled Subject and Contains.

5. **Click Subject and choose the part of the message that the program can use to identify messages.**

   For example, if you want to identify all messages from your mother, set this option to Sender.

6. **Click Contains and look at your other options. Chances are that you want to leave this option set to Contains.**

   Your other options include Doesn't Contain, Is, Isn't, Begins With, Ends With, Is In My Address Book, and Isn't In My Address Book.

7. **Click the box to the right of the last box and type the text you're looking for.**

   For example, type your mom's address.

8. **If you want to specify multiple criteria, click the More button.**

   Another Sender/Contains line appears. Repeat Steps 5–7 to create another criterion. You can keep clicking More to get additional criterion lines.

   For example, another way to identify messages from your mom is that they end with "Love, Mom."

9. **If *all* the criteria must be true for the message to fit your specs, choose Match All Of The Following. Otherwise, leave Match Any Of The Following selected.**

   This selection means that the filter finds messages that match any one or more of the criteria.

10. **Click Move To Folder on the Perform These Actions list.**

    Or, choose one of the other options, which include Delete The Message (probably not a good idea for messages from your mother).

11. **Click the drop-down button to the right of Move To Folder and choose Local Folders and then the folder to which you want to move the matching messages.**

12. **Click OK.**

    You go back to the Message Filters dialog box. You can start over at Step 3 if you want to create more filters.

13. **Click the X button in the upper-right corner of the dialog box to close it.**

The Netscape/Mozilla Mail built-in junk mail controls generally work better than creating your own filters, but you can always do both. After enabling the junk mail controls, you can create filters to move specific kinds of messages to your Junk, Trash, or other folders.

Chapter 8

Filtering Spam in Eudora

*E*udora has been around forever — we started using it in the early 1990s. Luckily, the people at Qualcomm have been updating it continually, and the latest version includes not only message filters you can make yourself, but also what they call SpamWatch — built-in Bayesian junk mail filters. Nice!

The reason that we like Eudora (well, one of the reasons) is that it isn't as susceptible to viruses as Outlook and Outlook Express. Also, it doesn't come bundled with a bunch of other software you may not want, as Netscape and Mozilla Mail are. If you use a Macintosh, consider Eudora because Mac versions are available.

If you want to try Eudora, you can download it from www.eudora.com. You can run it in Sponsored mode, which means that it's free, but it displays ads. Or, you can run it for free in Light mode, which omits some key features, including SpamWatch. Or, you can pay about $49 a year for Paid mode, in which you get all the features and no ads. Figure 8-1 shows Eudora 6 in Paid mode.

For help in getting Eudora up and running, refer to *The Internet For Dummies*, 9th Edition (Wiley Publishing, Inc.), by two of the same three authors — the Levines, specifically — who wrote this book.

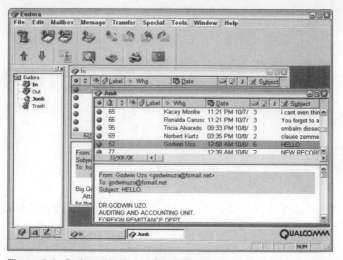

Figure 8-1: Eudora 6 includes SpamWatch, the Eudora junk mail filtering feature.

Watching Out for Spam with SpamWatch

The Eudora spam-filtering feature is named SpamWatch, and it uses *Bayesian filtering* (a method of spotting spam based on statistical analysis of the words in a message; see the sidebar "Bayesian what?" in Chapter 1). Each incoming message gets a *junk score* from 0 to 100. Higher scores mean that the message is more likely to be spam because it contains spam-like formatting or words. You can choose how aggressive or conservative SpamWatch should be by choosing the *junk threshold* — the junk score above which Eudora considers a message to be spam. Eudora starts with the threshold set at 50, and you can move it higher or lower to catch more or less spam.

Configuring SpamWatch

When you install Eudora, it may ask whether you want to use the Eudora Junk mailbox (folder), as shown in Figure 8-2. This question is the Eudora way of asking whether you want to turn

SpamWatch on. Clicking Yes in response to this message tells Eudora to create a mailbox (mail folder) named Junk and to turn on SpamWatch filtering.

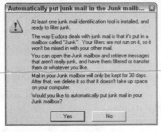

Figure 8-2: Do you want to turn on SpamWatch?

If you never saw this question, or if you answered No, all is not lost. You can turn it on by changing a few configuration settings. Even if you clicked Yes to turn SpamWatch on, you may want to check or change the settings. Follow these steps:

1. **Choose Tools⇨Options from the Eudora menu.**

   You see the Options dialog box, with a long list of categories down the left side.

2. **Scroll down to the Junk Mail category and select it.**

   You see the Junk Mail category of options, as shown in Figure 8-3.

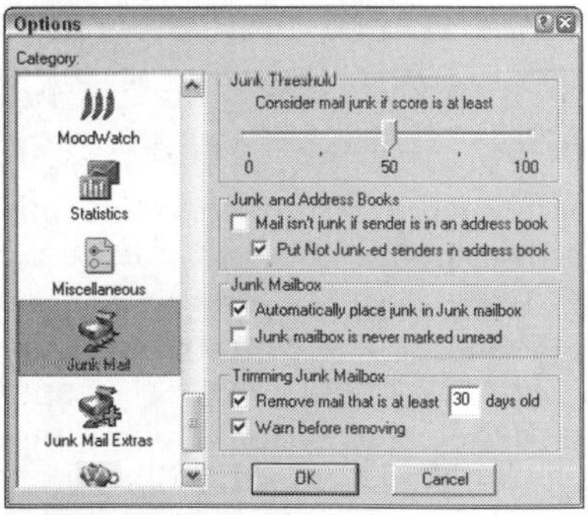

Figure 8-3: The Eudora Junk Mail (a.k.a. SpamWatch) settings.

3. **Adjust the Junk Threshold setting as needed.**

   If you're just starting out, leave it at 50. If SpamWatch has been getting *false positives* (treating good messages as spam), move the slider to the left to a lower number. If SpamWatch has been missing lots of spam, move the slider to the right to a higher number.

   We suggest that you leave the junk threshold alone for a week or two after starting to use SpamWatch. The program learns more about how to identify spam as you tell it which good messages are junk and which junk messages are spam, as described in the next section.

4. **Click to select the Mail Isn't Junk If Sender Is In An Address Book check box, unless you expect to get spam from friends.**

   For most people, messages from people in your address book are never junk. However, your mileage may vary!

5. **Clear the Put Not Junk-ed Senders In Address Book check box (click it until it's empty).**

   This option creates a new entry for every nonspam message you receive. We get lots of messages from people we don't expect to correspond with, so we prefer to turn this setting off. However, if you receive messages only from buddies, you may want to leave it selected.

   Note that Eudora ignores this setting if the option Mail Isn't Junk If Sender Is In An Address Book isn't selected.

6. **Select the Automatically Place Junk In Junk Mailbox check box so that it contains a check mark.**

   The whole *point* of spam filtering, in our humble opinions, is to get the spam out of our inboxes! If this check box isn't selected, Eudora marks suspected spam with an icon and leaves it in your In folder. We prefer to let Eudora move all suspected spam to the Junk folder and then review the Junk folder every few days, looking for false positives.

7. **Leave the Junk Mailbox Is Never Marked Unread check box unselected.**

   Selecting this check box means that even if new messages have been shunted into the Junk mailbox,

Eudora doesn't open the mailbox or display it in bold. We prefer to know when Eudora has junked messages, until we can get around to looking them over.

8. **Leave the Remove Mail That Is At Least ___ Days Old check box selected.**

There's no point keeping old spam. This setting tells Eudora when to move messages from the Junk folder to the Trash folder.

9. **Leave the Warn Before Removing check box selected.**

If you clear this check box, Eudora doesn't say anything when it clears out old messages from your Junk mailbox. Later, when you have SpamWatch trained so that it reliably spots spam, you may want to turn this option off.

A category named Junk Mail Extras contains some truly arcane settings (they're labeled Esoteric Stuff in our version of Eudora), but we recommend leaving them alone.

10. **Click OK to close the Options dialog box.**

Now, SpamWatch is up and running — it's rating each message as possible spam and moving to your Junk mailbox any messages with a rating of 50 or more.

Checking your Junk folder

SpamWatch examines each incoming message to determine whether it's naughty or nice. The naughty ones go into your Junk folder (assuming that you choose the Automatically Place Junk In Junk Mailbox option in the preceding section).

If the Junk mailbox isn't already open, display it by choosing Mailbox⇨Junk. The Junk Score column (usually the second column, right after the one with the big blue dots for unread messages) shows you the number from 1 to 100 (refer to Figure 8-1, earlier in this chapter).

At first, SpamWatch does a lousy of job of guessing which messages are spam; your In mailbox may contain lots of junk, and your Junk mailbox may contain lots of good messages. SpamWatch doesn't do as bad a job as many other filters right out of the box, though; it appears to start with a dictionary of words that traditionally appear in spam.

But you can train SpamWatch to do better. Training consists of looking in your Junk mailbox and telling Eudora which messages aren't spam and looking in your In mailbox (and any other mailboxes that contain incoming mail) and telling Eudora which messages are truly spam.

Look down the Subject lines of the messages in the Junk folder. Because spammers use deceptive Subject lines, you may need to select or open messages to tell whether they're spam. For messages that *aren't* spam, select the message and choose Message⇨Not Junk (or press Ctrl+Shift+J). Leave the rest of the spam in your Junk folder untouched; Eudora gets rid of it after it has hung around for 30 days. If you would rather not let the spam fester that long, you can select the messages and click the Delete Messages button on the toolbar, choose Message⇨Delete, or press Ctrl+D.

Marking spam that SpamWatch missed

The next step is to look at the messages in your In mailbox — you're probably about ready to look at them anyway because those messages are the whole point of having e-mail. For each message that is truly spam, select the message and either choose Message⇨Junk or press Ctrl+J. The message vanishes to your Junk mailbox, and Eudora makes a note of the words in the message, learning that messages with these words are likely to be spam.

If you have filters that move incoming messages to other mailboxes (as described in the next two sections), check these mailboxes too, for possible spam.

Are you curious about the junk scores of the messages in your In mailbox? You can display the junk score of messages in all your mailboxes, not just in the Junk mailbox. Choose Tools⇨ Options, select the Mailboxes category, select the Junk check box in the Show Mailbox Columns section of the dialog box, and click OK. While you're at it, you may want to clear the check boxes for columns you would rather not see, like Priority, Label, and Size.

Moving Messages into Eudora Mailboxes

Eudora SpamWatch works pretty well after it's trained, but you may want to create filters that spot specific types of messages and move them to your Junk mailbox (or other mailboxes). We use lots of filters, sorting our incoming mail into a separate mailbox for each mailing list we're on, along with a mailbox for News (various daily newspapers and newsletters).

Note that what other e-mail programs call *folders*, Eudora calls *mailboxes*. Same difference!

Creating Eudora mailboxes

Eudora comes with In, Out, Trash, and Junk folders (Junk is new in Eudora 6). To make a new folder, choose Mailbox⇨New from the menu and type a mailbox name. Then click OK.

You can also organize your mailboxes into folders (like files in directories). To create a folder in which to store mailboxes, choose Mailbox⇨New, type the folder name, click the Make It A Folder check box, and click OK.

"What mailboxes do I have?" you may ask. To see a list of your folders, choose Tools⇨Mailboxes. A mailbox list appears on the left side of the Eudora window. To close it, click the X in the upper-right corner of the list.

Creating Eudora filters to trash spam

To tell Eudora to sort your incoming messages into mailboxes, you create filters (the concepts behind filtering are described in Chapter 5). To see and create filters, choose Tools⇨Filters. You see the Filters dialog box, as shown in Figure 8-4. The existing filters are listed down the left side of the dialog box, and the details of the selected filter appear on the right side. The details are in two sections: Match (which messages the filter should catch) and Action (what to do with the messages).

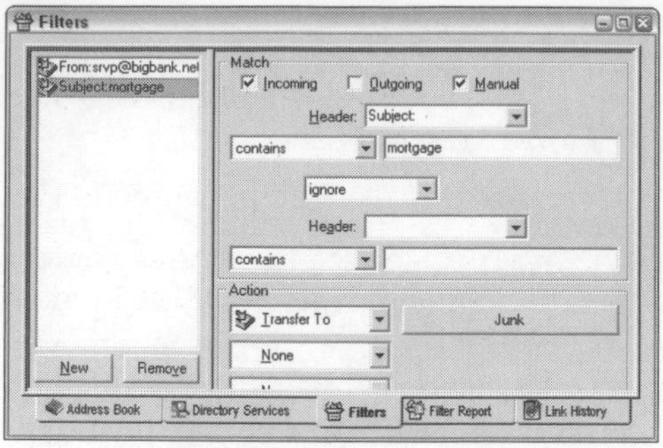

Figure 8-4: Eudora filters can move messages to the Junk mailbox (or any other mailbox) based on sender or addressee or words elsewhere in the message.

Pegasus: An excellent, free e-mail program with built-in spam filtering

If you like Eudora, you'll probably like Pegasus too. And Pegasus goes Eudora one better: It's completely free. Pegasus has no Paid or Sponsored modes. It's just plain free, and you can download it from www.pmail.com. We don't have space to describe how to install Pegasus, but the instructions on the Pegasus Web site should do the trick. If you decide to use Pegasus, please consider making a donation to its creator, or buying the documentation, to keep the program free.

David Harris, the creator of Pegasus, claims to have invented mail filtering in 1991. We disagree because one of the authors of this book (John) was filtering e-mail with his crusty old Unix-based e-mail programs way before 1991 — before PCs, in fact.

But Pegasus has had message filters longer than any other Windows e-mail program that we know of, and recent versions ship with a set of filters that can be used against spam.

To turn on spam filtering, choose Tools⇨Content Control, select the Basic Spam Detection testing set (the set of filters), click the Enable button, and click Done. Pegasus now uses its filters to move suspected spam to the Junk Or Suspicious Mail folder.

The Pegasus Content Control feature includes *blacklists* (lists of addresses from which all messages should be junked), *whitelists* (addresses from which no messages should be trashed), and *rules* (words considered in creating a *weight*, which is equivalent to the Eudora junk score).

Making a new filter is easy:

1. **Click the New button in the Filters dialog box to create a new, blank filter.**

   All you have to do now is fill in all the blanks!

2. **Click the Manual check box so that you can run the filter on existing messages, not just on incoming ones.**

   When the Manual option is selected, you can select a bunch of messages in a mailbox and choose Special⇨ Filter Messages to run your filters on those messages at any time.

3. **Set the Header drop-down box to the part of the message in which you want Eudora to look.**

   Your options are To (addressee), From (sender), Subject, Cc, Reply-to (not always the same as the From line), Any Header, Body (the text of the message), Any Recipient (any of the addresses that received this message), Personality (the e-mail account you use to create or receive the message), or Junk Score.

   Some third-party spam-filtering software adds a special header to spam messages: For example, POPFile (described in Chapter 11) can add an `X-Text-Classification: spam` header to messages it has marked as spam. POPFile users can use the Any Header option in your Eudora filter to move these messages into your Junk folder.

4. **In the blank box to the right of the Contains box, type the text or address you want to match the text or address you want to match.**

   For example, if you set the Header box to Subject, you can type **mortgage** to match all messages that mention mortgages on their Subject lines.

   You can change the Contains setting if you want to match all messages that *don't* contain specific text or other, more arcane situations.

5. **To specify a second criterion for this filter, change the Ignore box to And, Or, or Unless. Then select the second Header box and type the text or address for the second criterion to match.**

For example, you may not want to trash messages that mention mortgages if they're from your bank. You can set the Ignore box to Unless, set the second Header to From, and type the bank's address in the box to the right of the second Contains box.

You're done with the Match section of the filter. On to the Action section! You can specify as many as five actions, which is why you see five boxes labeled None. You change the None setting to the action that you want Eudora to take.

6. **Click the first None box and set it to Junk.**

   If you're filtering messages for a purpose other than spam-trashing, you can choose any of the other options. For example, if you're creating a filter to move messages from a mailing list to a separate mailbox, you would choose Transfer To at this point. For some choices, additional boxes, blanks, or check boxes appear to the right of the None box, so you can specify more information about the action. For junking a message, no other information is necessary.

7. **Click the X box in the upper-right corner to close the Filters dialog box, and click Yes to save your changes.**

When you're reading a message, you can use the Special⇨ Make Filter command to create a new filter that moves all messages from this sender to a new mailbox with the name of the sender.

Chapter 9

Filtering Spam in AOL and AOL Communicator

• •

In This Chapter

▶ Setting AOL to throw spam out, at least some of it

▶ Running AOL Communicator Mail

▶ Setting the AOL Communicator Mail junk mail settings

▶ Creating folders and filters in AOL Communicator Mail

▶ Configuring Netscape Mail to work with AOL

• •

America Online (AOL) has been a leader in fighting spam, but AOL provides such an attractive target for spammers that it has been a losing battle. Luckily, AOL users have several options:

 ✔ Use the regular AOL software to read your e-mail. You don't have many filtering options, but you may as well as configure those that are available. This chapter describes AOL 9.0 spam and mail controls.

 ✔ Read your messages using AOL Communicator, a free e-mail program that works with AOL. This chapter describes how to get AOL Communicator and set it up, including its spam filters.

 ✔ Use Netscape 7 to read your mail, with its built-in filtering (described at the end of this chapter and in Chapter 7).

Our advice is to download and install AOL Communicator! It's a fine mail program, and not just for its spam filtering.

Fighting Spam in AOL 9

AOL filters out and throws away over a billion (that's billion with a *b*) spam messages every day. It has a full-time staff of spam-fighters who write, test, and install new filters all the time. However, lots of spam still gets through because even a little bit of a billion messages is a great deal of spam.

Setting your AOL spam options

In the AOL 9.0 program, after you log in, choose Mail➪Block Unwanted Mail to display the Mail and Spam Controls dialog box, as shown in Figure 9-1.

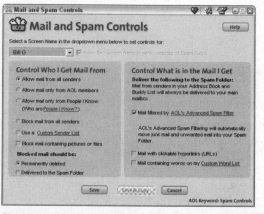

Figure 9-1: You can configure the AOL mail and spam controls.

In this dialog box, select the screen name for which you want to configure mail filters — you can use different filters for different screen names. Then select settings depending on what you want to do:

✔ **Receive mail only from people in your AOL address book and on your Buddy List:** Select the option Allow Mail Only From People I Know.

✔ **Specify addresses and domains to block:** Select Use a Custom Sender List and click the Custom Sender List link. In the Custom Sender List dialog box, type addresses or domain names and click Add after each one. Then click Save.

✔ **Avoid mail with graphics or attached files:** Select the Block Mail Containing Pictures Or Files check box.

✔ **Use the AOL Spam Filter:** You may as well use AOL spam filtering, so leave the Mail Filtered By AOL Advanced Spam Filter check box selected.

✔ **Avoid mail that contains specific words:** You can create a list of words you don't want to hear about. Select the option Mail Containing Words On My Custom Word List and click the Custom Word List link. In the Custom Word List dialog box that opens, type your words and click Add after each one. Then click Save.

After you have told AOL what mail to block, specify what to do with blocked messages. Select the option Delivered To The Spam Folder so that you can look through the messages from time to time.

After you have set your mail-filtering options, click Save.

If you have screen names your children use, set their mail filtering to Allow Mail Only From People I Know and add their friends and relatives to their address books.

Creating folders for your mail

AOL can store messages in mail folders on your own computer rather than on the AOL mail servers. Follow these steps:

1. **Click the Read icon on the AOL toolbar.**

   The Mailbox window opens.

2. **Select the Manage Mail tab.**

3. **On the My Mail Folders list on the left, scroll down and select Saved On My PC.**

   You see a list of the AOL mail folders on your computer, including Incoming/Saved Mail, Mail Waiting To Be Sent, and Mail You've Sent.

4. **Click the Setup Folders button and select Create Folder.**

   You see a little Create New Folder dialog box.

5. **Type a name for your folder and click Save.**

After you have created folders, you can store messages in them. With a message selected, click the Save button and select On My PC and then the name of the folder.

However, AOL doesn't let you create filters that automatically move messages to folders. For that task, you need to use a better e-mail program, so keep reading!

Junking Spam in AOL Communicator Mail

The free AOL Communicator program includes AOL Communicator Mail, the AOL customized version of Netscape Mail, as well as instant messaging and Radio@AOL — easy access to streaming radio stations over the Internet. Its e-mail program has many of the same commands and functions as Netscape Mail, which is described in Chapter 7. The initial version of AOL Communicator runs on Windows, and a Mac version is coming.

One great thing about AOL Communicator Mail is that it includes Bayesian spam filtering, just like Netscape 7.1 does. (Because AOL owns Netscape, it's probably the same filter.) You can train AOL Communicator Mail to throw away lots of spam that gets through the AOL server-based filters.

Getting AOL Communicator

If you want to download the program and try it, you can find it at www.aol.com/downloads or AOL keyword **AOL Communicator**. Follow the instructions on the Web site to download the program file (ac_install.exe) and then install it. The program steps you through a configuration process.

After you install the program, you can start it by choosing Start⇨Programs⇨AOL Communicator⇨AOL Communicator or double-clicking its icon on your desktop. Both the mail and instant messaging windows pop up: Just close the IM window if you don't plan to use it.

AOL Communicator doesn't connect you to AOL or to the Internet. You need to use your usual method — the AOL program or another connection program — to get online.

You can use AOL Communicator Mail for your AOL e-mail, as well as for e-mail from most other accounts (except Hotmail and MSN and other Web-based accounts). After AOL Communicator is running, it looks like Figure 9-2.

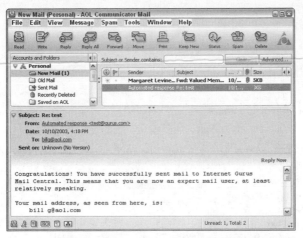

Figure 9-2: AOL Communicator Mail is a big improvement over the AOL built-in e-mail handling, including better spam blocking.

Don't try to use other e-mail programs with AOL, because they don't work. Most normal e-mail programs work with POP and IMAP mail servers (the standard types of Internet mail server), and AOL runs its servers with its own proprietary protocols. Only AOL Communicator and Netscape 7 work directly with AOL.

Blocking spam in AOL Communicator Mail

Isn't it refreshing to see a Spam command right on your e-mail program's toolbar? No, it's not for *sending* spam — it's for blocking it (but you probably already guessed that).

When you install AOL Communicator, its spam filters are turned off for your AOL mail and turned on for any other (POP or IMAP) e-mail accounts you set up. To turn on spam filtering for your AOL messages, follow these steps:

1. **Choose Spam⇨Spam Filter.**

   You see the Spam Filter dialog box, as shown in Figure 9-3.

Figure 9-3: Turn on spam filtering for your AOL account.

2. **If the Filter Spam For All Accounts option isn't selected, click it.**

   Your alternative is to select Only For The Selected Accounts Below and then select from the list, but why not filter everything?

3. **Click to select the Options tab in the dialog box.**

   You see a few more options.

4. **If the check box labeled Messages From People In My Address Book Are Never Spam isn't selected, click it.**

   If you're like us, you want to read all messages from people you know, unless you hang around with lots of spammers.

5. **Select the Auto-Delete Spam 1 Week After I Receive It check box.**

   If you collect antique spam, don't select this option. If you're worried about deleting good messages that get misidentified as spam, be sure to check your spam folder, as described in the section "Showing, hiding, and deleting spam," later in this chapter. You may also want to change 1 Week to 2 Weeks to give yourself more time to sift through your spam for false positives.

6. **Click OK.**

The Reset Spam Filter button on the Options tab of the Spam Filter dialog box wipes out all training you have already provided; that is, it empties the *corpus* of spam information that the filters have been accumulating.

Training your spam filters

At first, the AOL Communicator Mail spam filters don't spot much spam because you need to train them to identify it. On the list of incoming messages, an icon identifies each message as okay (a sun) or spam (envelopes sticking out of a trash can, like you see in the margin).

If (when) AOL Communicator Mail misses a piece of spam (that is, a spam message doesn't have a spam icon), correct it by selecting, or opening, the message and clicking the Spam button on the toolbar. The button has the same envelopes-in-the-trash spam icon.

Conversely, AOL Communicator Mail may mark a good message as spam. If so, select the message and choose Spam⇨Mark As Not Spam, right-click the message, and choose Mark As Not Spam from the menu that appears, or (our favorite method) click the This Is Not Spam button at the top of the message.

The more messages you tell the program about, the more accurate its filtering becomes — that's the genius of Bayesian filtering.

Showing, hiding, and deleting spam

You don't have to look at the spam in your New Mail folder; you can tell AOL Communicator Mail to hide it. Choose Spam⇨ Show Spam Messages to toggle between showing and hiding the messages that are marked as spam. We usually keep this option unselected so that no check mark appears by the Show Spam Messages command on the Spam menu and we don't have to deal with spam as we read our mail. But every few days, follow these steps to check and get rid of your spam messages:

1. **Select the New Mail folder on the Accounts And Folders list (it's probably already selected).**

2. **Choose Spam⇨Show Spam Messages to display your spam.**

   The messages are mixed in among your other messages.

3. **Scan down the messages that are marked as spam, looking for any that *aren't* spam. If you find any, select the message and choose Spam⇨Mark As Not Spam.**

   Now all the spam-marked messages really *are* spam.

4. **Choose Spam⇨Delete Spam from This Folder to blow the spam away.**

Creating folders in AOL Communicator Mail

Another way to avoid reading spam is to create folders for different sorts of messages and filters for moving suspected spam into a specific folder. Chapter 5 describes the general idea.

To create a folder in AOL Communicator Mail, follow these steps:

1. **Choose File⇨New⇨Folder.**

   You see the New Folder dialog box.

2. **Type a name for the folder in the Name box.**

   For example, you can make a folder named Suspected Spam.

   Leave the Create As A Subfolder Of option set to Local Mail.

3. **Click OK.**

   The folder appears in the Local Mail section of the Accounts And Folders list.

Now you have a place to move messages that you think are spam but that the AOL Communicator Mail spam filters are missing. You can move messages from one folder to another by hand, by either dragging them from the message list to another folder on the Accounts and Folders list or by right-clicking a message and choosing Move To and the folder name. But AOL Communicator Mail can move messages automatically if you create filters.

Creating filters in AOL Communicator Mail

When you create a filter, you tell AOL Communicator Mail what kinds of messages you want to work with and what to do with them. To create a filter that identifies spam containing specific words, follow these steps:

1. **Choose Tools⊅Custom Message Filters⊅Setup.**

   You see the Setup Custom Message Filters dialog box.

2. **Click the New Filter button.**

   The Custom Message Filter dialog box appears, as shown in Figure 9-4.

3. **Type a name in the Filter name box (it can be anything that reminds you what the filter is for).**

4. **On the Perform The Following Action line, set the rightmost box to the name of the folder to which you want to move the suspected spam.**

   You can move it right to the Trash folder, but a safer method is to move it to a Suspected Spam folder that you check and empty from time to time.

Figure 9-4: Filter your incoming messages into folders by subject, content, or sender or by other information.

The lower part of the dialog box contains the condition(s) that have to be met for AOL Communicator Mail to apply the filter to a message. At first, one condition appears, saying the subject of the message contains ___.

5. **Set the first drop-down box on the Condition line to the part of the message you want the filter to look at.**

   You can select Subject, Sender, Date, Status, To, Cc, or Recipient.

6. **Set the second drop-down box on the condition line to how the match should work.**

   Your options are Contains, Doesn't contain, Is, Isn't, Begins with, or Ends with.

7. **In the rightmost box on the condition line, type the text to match.**

   Figure 9-4 shows a filter that matches any message whose subject contains the word *mortgage*.

8. **If you want multiple conditions for the filter, click the Add + button to add another condition line, and then repeat Steps 5–7 to create the new condition. Also set the drop-down box in the line above the first condition to either Any or All.**

   The line above the first condition line says If Any of the following conditions are met, but you can change Any to All.

9. **Click OK to save the filter.**

You can create lots of filters, including filters that sort mailing-list and newsletter messages into separate folders.

Using Netscape to Read Your AOL Mail

If you already use Netscape 7 Mail and you don't feel like converting over to AOL Communicator Mail, you can configure Netscape Mail to work with your AOL messages. In Netscape Mail, follow these steps:

1. **Choose Edit⇨Mail & Newsgroups Account Settings.**

   You see the Mail & Newsgroups Account Settings dialog box.

2. **Click the Add Account button.**

   The Account Wizard runs.

3. **On the first Account Wizard screen, select AOL account as the type of account. Click Next.**

4. **Type your name and your AOL screen name where indicated and click Next.**

   Omit the spaces from your screen name when you type it.

5. **Click Finish and OK.**

   Now AOL Mail appears on the folder list on the left side of the Netscape Mail window and contain one folder — your AOL Inbox.

Refer to Chapter 7 to find out how to filter out spam using Netscape 7.

Chapter 10

Filtering Spam in Hotmail, MSN, and Yahoo! Mail

● ●

In This Chapter

▶ Setting Hotmail and MSN spam options

▶ Reading your Hotmail or MSN mail with Outlook Express or other e-mail programs

▶ Setting Yahoo! Mail junk mail filter options

▶ Reading your Yahoo! Mail messages with a real e-mail program

● ●

*M*any *Web-based* mail systems exist — mailboxes you use by going to a Web site, logging in, and reading and sending messages by using your Web browser. Hotmail was the first Web-based mail system we know of, but dozens are now available, including Yahoo! Mail (owned by the popular Yahoo! Web directory). The Microsoft MSN service uses Hotmail for its mail, so everything we say about Hotmail applies to MSN mail too. This chapter describes your spam-filtering options if you use Hotmail, MSN, or Yahoo! Mail accounts.

You can follow two basic approaches:

✔ Turn on the spam filters that are built into Hotmail and Yahoo! Mail. Both these services do their best to move spam into a separate Junk Mail folder.

✔ Rather than read your messages via a Web browser, download your Hotmail or Yahoo! Mail messages into a real e-mail program, like Netscape Mail, Eudora, or Outlook Express. Then use your e-mail program's spam filters.

We recommend using both these approaches to minimize the amount of spam you have to put up with.

Spam Options for Hotmail and MSN Users

Hotmail and MSN mail filter out tons of spam, although you probably still get a fair amount. The next section explains how to make sure that Hotmail or MSN is throwing away as much spam as it can identify.

You have several options for reading your Hotmail or MSN messages:

✔ Go to the www.hotmail.com or www.msn.com Web site and use its Web-based system.

✔ Set up Outlook Express or Outlook to download your Hotmail or MSN messages.

✔ Set up another e-mail program (like Netscape Mail or Eudora) to read your Hotmail or MSN messages.

Later sections in this chapter describe how to reduce spam by using Outlook Express, Outlook, or another e-mail program rather than reading your mail on the Web.

 Several third-party spam-filtering programs, including InBoxCop (www.inboxcop.com), work with Hotmail or MSN (see Chapter 11).

Setting your Hotmail or MSN spam options

Hotmail and MSN can spot some spam and move it out of your Inbox folder and into a separate Junk Mail folder.

After you log in at www.hotmail.com or www.msn.com, select the Options tab. (It may not look like a tab, but it appears on a row with a bunch of tabs, so we assume that it's a tab.) Hotmail and MSN list several spam-related options you can click to configure, as shown in Figure 10-1:

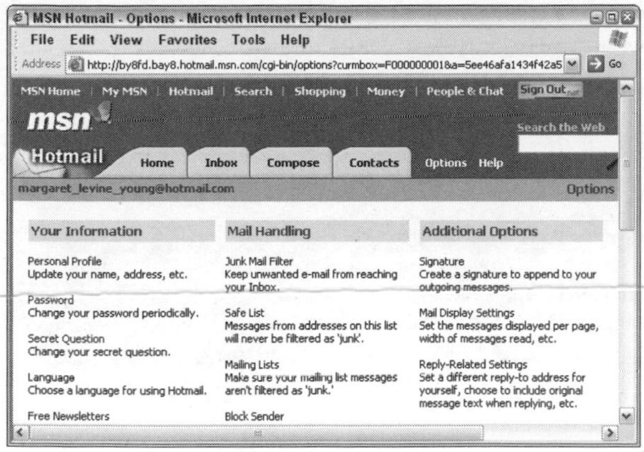

Figure 10-1: Hotmail and MSN have built-in junk mail filters.

✔ **Junk Mail Filter:** Selects the Junk Mail Filter level. Your choices are Default, Enhanced (catches more spam, but may mislabel more good mail as spam), and Exclusive (filters out all messages except those from people on your Contacts list, Hotmail administration itself, and MSN announcements you have signed up for). If you get lots of spam, try setting your filters to Enhanced.

✔ **Safe List:** Creates a list of addresses or domains from which messages are never filtered as spam. If you work at an organization with a domain name (for example, you work at Joe's Bank with the domain name joesbank. com), you may want to put your organization's domain on the Safe List so that no messages from coworkers are ever considered to be spam.

✔ **Mailing Lists:** Creates a list of addresses that appear on the To line of messages that aren't spam. Most messages you receive have *your* address on the To line, but not all of them. Many e-mail mailing lists send messages with the list address (rather than your address) in the To header.

✔ **Block Sender:** Creates a list of addresses or domains for which *all* messages are marked as spam.

✔ **Custom Filters:** Creates filters that move messages that match your criteria to a folder or into the trash, as shown in Figure 10-2. Click the Create New button to make a filter. (Refer to Chapter 5 for the concepts behind creating mail filters.)

Figure 10-2: You can create your own filters in Hotmail and MSN.

Hotmail and MSN come with Inbox and Junk Mail folders, but you can create additional folders in which to store your mail. To make a new folder, select the Home tab, click the View All Folders link, and click the Create New button. To move a message to a folder, select or display a message, click the Put In Folder pull-down button, and select the folder name from the menu that appears. Or, select one or more messages from your Inbox by selecting their check boxes and then click the Put In Folder button.

Reading Hotmail or MSN mail from Outlook Express or Outlook

Hotmail and MSN use a proprietary mailbox protocol rather than the industry standard POP and IMAP, so most e-mail programs can't read or send mail directly via Hotmail or MSN. (See the next section for workarounds, though.) Outlook, Outlook Express, Hotmail, and MSN all come from Microsoft, so it's not too surprising that they work together.

Follow these steps to configure Outlook 2002, Outlook 2003, or Outlook Express to read and send messages via your Hotmail or MSN account (Outlook 2000 doesn't work with Hotmail):

1. **In Outlook Express, choose Tools⇨Accounts, click the Add button, and choose Mail from the menu that appears. In Outlook, choose Tools⇨E-Mail Accounts and choose Add A New E-Mail Account.**

   A wizard runs. Answer the wizard's questions and click Next to move from screen to screen.

2. **When the wizard asks about server types, change POP3 to HTTP as the type of server (in Outlook Express) or click HTTP (in Outlook).**

   HTTP (or HyperText Transfer Protocol, to be precise) is the protocol that Web browsers use to talk to Web servers.

3. **Set the My HTTP Mail Server Provider Is or HTTP Mail Service Provider box to Hotmail.**

4. **Answer the rest of the questions, clicking Next as needed, and then click Finish.**

   If you use Outlook, you're done.

5. **In Outlook Express, click Close to dismiss the Internet Accounts dialog box.**

   Outlook Express asks whether you want to download folders from the mail server you just added (Hotmail).

6. **Click Yes.**

Now Hotmail and its various folders appear on your Folders list. Refer to Chapter 6 to find how to set up spam filtering in Outlook and Outlook Express.

Reading Hotmail or MSN mail with any old e-mail program

In theory, you can't use other e-mail programs (like Netscape Mail or Eudora) to read Hotmail messages because Hotmail doesn't use any Internet standard protocol. Instead, it uses a proprietary Microsoft protocol (Microsoft avoids following standards because, as far as we can tell, it would rather force you to use its products than to let you have a choice of programs.)

However, the free program Hotmail Popper (from www.boolean.ca/hotpop) makes Hotmail look like a standard POP (Post Office Protocol) server, from which most e-mail programs can retrieve messages. For example, you can use Hotmail Popper and Eudora 6, an e-mail program with good spam filtering, to read and send Hotmail messages.

Spam Options for Yahoo! Mail Users

Yahoo! Mail is our favorite Web-based mail system. You use it by pointing your Web browser at mail.yahoo.com and signing up for a free account. Like Hotmail and MSN, Yahoo! Mail includes spam filtering. You can also use other e-mail programs to read and send messages via Yahoo! Mail.

When you read the messages in your Yahoo! Mail inbox, if you see a spam message, click the Spam button rather than the Delete button. The Spam button educates Yahoo! Mail about what your spam looks like so that it can do a better job of spotting it and directing it into your Bulk (junk mail) folder.

Setting your Yahoo! Mail filtering options

The Yahoo! Mail spam-filtering system is SpamGuard, and you don't need to turn it on or configure it. SpamGuard moves messages that look like spam into your Bulk folder. After 30 days, these messages are deleted. You should check your Bulk folder every week or so to look for *false positives* — good messages that have gotten lumped in with the spam. If you find one, click its Not Spam button.

To configure the Yahoo! Mail filters, sign in and click the <u>Mail Options</u> link. Then click one of these four links:

- ✔ **Spam Protection:** You can turn SpamGuard on or off and your SpamGuard options.

- ✔ **Anti-Spam Resource Center:** This link takes you to the Yahoo! Mail pages about spam and how to avoid it.

- ✔ **Block Addresses:** You can specify addresses or domains from which you don't want to receive mail. Yahoo! Mail moves those messages right into the trash.

- ✔ **Filters:** You can create filters that move messages matching your criteria out of your Inbox folder and into another folder (which can be the Trash folder). Click Add to create a new filter (you can have as many as 15). Fill out the form shown in Figure 10-3 and click the Add Filter button.

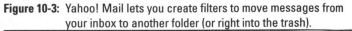

Figure 10-3: Yahoo! Mail lets you create filters to move messages from your inbox to another folder (or right into the trash).

To create folders in Yahoo! Mail, click the <u>Add</u> link to the right of the <u>Folders</u> link on the main Yahoo! Mail page.

Reading Yahoo! Mail with another e-mail program

Yahoo! offers POP access for $20 per year. You can download Yahoo! Mail messages into an e-mail program like Netscape Mail, Eudora, or Outlook Express. We like this idea because you can then use the additional spam filters in these programs. However, we're not crazy about paying $20 a year (although now that we think of it, that's not much money for the convenience of less spam).

An alternative is to use a free program named YahooPOPs to provide POP access to Yahoo! Mail. You can download it from `yahoopops.sourceforge.net`.

Part III

Spam-Filtering Programs and Services

The 5th Wave   By Rich Tennant

"I like getting junk mail by e-mail. It's easier to delete than to shred."

In this part . . .

*F*ew e-mail programs include truly effective spam filters. This part of the book describes some additional
ways you can get the spam out of your inbox, including
installing extra spam-filtering software and signing up for
spam-filtering services. We have been amazed at how
effective spam-filtering software has become — some
great spam filters are even available for free!

And we have something for the geeks among you, too. For
people who run mail servers (the Internet server computers that store mailboxes), Chapter 13 talks about server-
based spam-fighting systems.

Chapter 11

A Round-Up of Desktop Antispam Programs

. . . .

In This Chapter

▶ Why you should install a spam filter?

▶ Lots of spam filtering programs to consider

▶ POPFile: the people's spam filter

▶ Spam Bully, a program that plugs into Outlook and Outlook Express

. . . .

A gaggle of spam-fighting programs are on the market. We have been amazed to see how many send out spam to suggest that you buy them: Isn't that a bit like your doctor infecting you with influenza so that he can provide the antibiotic to cure it?

However, some antispam programs are worth their weight in gold. This chapter reviews a few spam-filtering programs that run under Windows and trap spam even before your e-mail program receives it.

Chapter 12 describes ISPs and other services you can subscribe to if you don't want to install antispam software on your computer. Chapter 13 is for the geeks who run mail servers, corporate networks, and ISPs and need large-scale, hard-core, server-based spam-filtering solutions.

Keep in mind that filtering your e-mail doesn't make the problem of spam go away. Your ISP still receives, processes, and delivers thousands, millions, or even billions of unwanted e-mails. Just because you may get good results in filtering doesn't mean that the costs of all those extra servers and Internet connections aren't being passed along to you. Just remember that although filters may help you win your daily spam battles, the war against spammers is bigger and more costly than you can imagine.

Most E-Mail Programs Can't Go It Alone

Part II describes the spam-filtering features of the major e-mail programs, and frankly, only two of the programs do much to rid your inbox of spam. If your e-mail program doesn't have spam-filtering features built in, consider switching to one that does or installing a third-party program that specializes in snagging spam.

The exceptions to this statement are Netscape, Mozilla, and Eudora, which have advanced filtering built in. Netscape Mail (starting with Version 7.1) and Mozilla Mail (starting with Version 1.3), which we describe in Chapter 7, already include the type of spam-spotting that stand-alone spam filters like POPFile provide. Eudora 6 does too (refer to Chapter 8).

How third-party programs work

Many of these programs act as *proxy servers* —programs that stand between you and the Internet (in this case, between your e-mail program and your ISP's mail server). Instead of your e-mail program getting the mail from the mail server directly, the spam filter program gets your messages from the mail server and throws out most of the spam, and then your e-mail program gets your messages from your spam filter program. Yes, it's an extra step, but lots of spam can disappear along the way.

Table 11-1 lists some popular and effective spam-filtering programs you can install on Windows, UNIX, or Linux systems or on the Mac. Table 11-2 lists programs that work with only Outlook or Outlook Express.

Because new versions of these programs come out all the time (they have to, in order to stay ahead of the spammers), we don't include step-by-step instructions for all these programs. Instead, we describe one stand-alone program (POPFile) and one Outlook Express add-in (Spam Bully) in detail, so you get the idea. Other programs work similarly.

Table 11-1   Stand-Alone Spam Filters

Program	URL	Comments
InBoxCop	www.inboxcop.com	Works with Web mail accounts, such as Hotmail, MSN, and Yahoo! Mail, and with AOL. Adds Bayesian filtering and checks messages against lists of known spam. Free for one computer with one account.
K9	www.keir.net/k9.html	POP accounts only; adds Bayesian filter. Freeware.
Lyris MailShield Desktop	www.lyris.com/products/mailshield/desktop	POP, IMAP, Hotmail, and MSN accounts; adds Bayesian filtering.
MailWasher and MailWasher Pro	www.mailwasher.net	Free and paid versions. Both support POP accounts with Bayesian filtering and Web-based blacklists. Paid version supports Hotmail and MSN accounts.

(continued)

Table 11-1 *(continued)*

Program	URL	Comments
POPFile	popfile.sourceforge.net	Cross-platform (but you have to install Perl), open source freeware using Bayesian filtering and whitelists.
Saproxy Pro	www.statalabs.com/products/saproxy/overview.php	POP accounts only. Based on SpamAssassin (described in Chapter 13). Includes Bayesian filtering.
SayNoToSpam	www.saynotospam.com	Includes virus-checking; for POP accounts only. Uses whitelisting and Bayesian filters and has an online database of spam that is updated hourly.
SpamBayes	spambayes.sourceforge.net	Open source implementation of Bayesian filtering for POP and IMAP accounts. Available for Windows, UNIX/Linux, and the Mac.
SpamButcher	www.spambutcher.com	For POP accounts only.
Spamihilator	www.spamihilator.com	Adds free Bayesian filtering for POP accounts.

Program	URL	Comments
Spam Inspector	www.spaminspector.com	Uses Bayesian filters, whitelists, and updates from community database of spam messages. Works with Outlook, Outlook Express, Eudora, IncrediMail, and Web-based Hotmail and MSN.
SpamPal	www.spampal.org	Freeware for POP and IMAP accounts only. Uses Bayesian filtering and blocking (DNSBL) lists; see Chapter 13.
SpamProbe	sourceforge.net/projects/ spamprobe	Open source, free Bayesian filtering for Unix/Linux and Mac OS X.
Spam Sleuth	www.bluesquirrel.com/ products/SpamSleuth	For POP accounts. Works with AOL, Hotmail, MSN, and Yahoo! Mail by bundling Web2POP utility. Uses Bayesian filters, challenge e-mails, whitelists, and blacklists.

Table 11-2 Add-Ins for Outlook and Outlook Express

Program	URL	Comments
GBS Inbox Protector	www.gbs-design.com/ inboxprotector	For Outlook and Outlook Express.
InBoxer	www.inboxer.com	Adds Bayesian filtering to Outlook, but not Outlook Express.

(continued)

Table 11-2 *(continued)*

Program	URL	Comments
MailFrontier Anti-Spam Matador	www.mailfrontier.com	For POP, IMAP, Hotmail, and MSN accounts. Uses Bayesian filters, whitelists, blacklists, and challenge e-mails that ask correspondents to identify themselves. For Outlook and Outlook Express.
Motino	www.angenous.com/motino	Adds Bayesian filtering to Outlook, but not Outlook Express.
POPFile with Outclass	popfile.sourceforge.net (for POPFile) www.vargonsoft.com/Outclass (for Outclass)	Allows POPFile to work with Outlook and POP, IMAP, and Exchange accounts. May not work with Hotmail and MSN. Not for Outlook Express.
SpamBayes Outlook Addin	spambayes.sourceforge.net/windows.html	Outlook add-in version of SpamBayes (refer to Table 11-1). Not for Outlook Express.
Spam Bully	www.spambully.com	Adds Bayesian filters for Outlook and Outlook Express. Can also auto-bounce spam messages, send challenge messages, and block attachments. Works with POP, IMAP, Hotmail, MSN, and Exchange accounts.
Spamnet for Outlook Express and Spamnet for Outlook	www.cloudmark.com	Community-based spam identification. No Bayesian filtering. Works with POP, Hotmail, and MSN accounts.

The latest on antispam programs

Spam programs are popping up like mushrooms after a spring rain, and by the time you read this chapter, another 50 may be available. A number of Web sites are devoted to listing and reviewing spam filters, including these:

✓ **Spamotomy** (www.spamotomy.com): Spam news and a listing of programs

✓ **About.com's Internet For Beginners Spam page** (www.netfor beginners.about.com/cs/spam): Tips and tricks

✓ **About.com's Email Anti-Spam Tools and Services page** (email.about. com/cs/antispamreviews)

✓ **WebAttack.com's Anti-Spam Tools page: Shareware** (www.webattack. com/shareware/comm/swspam.html)

✓ **WebAttack Internet Tools' Anti-Spam Tools: Freeware** (www. webattack.com/freeware/comm/fwspam.html): Ditto, for freeware (programs that are totally free)

Also check our Web site at privacy.gurus.com for news about spam.

What if you don't POP?

Many stand-alone spam filters work with only POP (also know as POP3, both of which are acronyms for Post Office Protocol) mail accounts. Luckily, this type of account is the type that 99 percent of ISPs provide. Here are other types of mail accounts, and what to do if you use them:

> ✓ **Hotmail and MSN:** Hotmail and MSN have a proprietary Web-based protocol. Luckily, you can configure Outlook Express and Outlook to work with them. Then install one of the spam filters listed in Table 11-2. InBoxCop (www.inboxcop.com) also works with Hotmail and MSN. Alternatively, you can install a free program named Hotmail Popper (from www.boolean.ca/hotpop), which provides POP access to Hotmail. InBoxCop, Lyris MailShield Desktop, MailWasher Pro, and Spam Sleuth (described in Table 11-1) all work with Hotmail and MSN.

✔ **Yahoo! Mail:** Yahoo! Mail is another Web-based mail system. Yahoo! provides POP access to your Yahoo! Mail account for $20 a year. To turn this option on, click Mail Options on the Yahoo! Mail Web page and then click the POP Access and Mail Forwarding link. Alternatively, you can try a free utility named YahooPOPs (at `yahoopops. sourceforge.net`). It claims to provide POP access to Yahoo! mailboxes, but may result in a confusing setup. InBoxCop and Spam Sleuth (described in Table 11-1) also work with Yahoo! Mail.

✔ **AOL:** You can use AOL Communicator Mail to read your AOL mail, and it includes Baysian filtering. InBoxCop and Spam Sleuth (described in Table 11-1) also work with AOL.

✔ **Lotus Notes:** Some large organizations use Lotus Notes for e-mail, calendars, and shared conferencing. POPFile works with Lotus Notes.

✔ **IMAP and Microsoft Exchange:** These types of mailboxes are used in many large organizations. The mailboxes allow you to read and send e-mail while leaving your messages on the central server, rather than download messages to your computer. Talk to your system administrator and tell her to read Chapter 13 of this book to provide server-level spam blocking. Some of the spam-blockers in Tables 11-1 and 11-2 work with IMAP accounts.

POPFile: The Open Source Spam Filter

POPFile is one of a number of powerful but simple programs that can greatly reduce the amount of spam that ends up in your inbox. POPFile is a *Bayesian* filter, a filter you train to tell the difference between spam and not spam based on experience. (See the "Bayesian what?" sidebar in Chapter 1.) This section of the chapter describes POPFile in some detail, although other Bayesian filtering programs work similarly.

POPFile provides a powerful tool for separating spam from good messages. Here's how it works:

1. POPFile retrieves your mail from your POP mail server, by pretending to be your e-mail program.

2. POPFile examines each message and tags those that appear to be spam with a special mail header or special words added to the Subject line.

3. Your regular e-mail program gets your mail from POPFile.

4. Using a rule that you create in your e-mail program, your program filters all the messages that POPFile tagged into a Suspected Spam folder or directly into the trash. (Part II describes how to create rules to filter incoming messages into a folder).

Although some e-mail programs (such as Outlook 2003) have elaborate spam-filtering rules, those rules aren't as sophisticated as POPFile's. By running as a stand-alone program, POPFile can work with almost any e-mail program. POPFile doesn't throw away spam; it *tags* it so that your e-mail program can throw it away.

If you use Netscape Mail 7.1 (or later), Mozilla Mail 1.5 (or later), or Eudora 6, you already have a Bayesian filtering program like POPFile built right in. Refer to Chapter 7 to find out how to turn on the Netscape and Mozilla junk mail controls. Chapter 8 describes the Eudora 6 spam filter. Just turn on these programs' junk mail controls and forget about POPFile.

How POPFile tags messages

When POPFile tags your messages, it marks them as belonging in a specific *bucket,* the POPFile equivalent of a folder. You should create at least two buckets: one for spam and one for everything else. Then you have two choices for how POPFile tags the messages for each bucket:

✔ **Adding a new header:** Every e-mail message contains lots of header lines showing its path from the sender to the receiver, although your e-mail program does you the favor of not displaying all of them. POPFile can add an extra header, named X-Text-Classification, that contains the name of the bucket the message is in. For example, if you tell POPFile to tag your messages by adding a header, it adds this line to the header of each message tagged for your Spam bucket:

```
X-Text-Classification: spam
```

> ✔ **Subject modification:** Alternatively, POPFile can add the bucket name to the beginning of the Subject heading for each message, like this:
>
> ```
> Subject: [spam] Eliminate Your Debt Now!
> ```

Which tagging system you use depends on which e-mail program you use. (See the chapter in Part II that describes your e-mail program.) Almost all e-mail programs can filter messages based on the Subject line text (for example, moving all messages with [spam] on the Subject line directly into your Deleted Items or Trash folder).

You can make as many buckets in POPFile as you like: It's not limited to looking for spam. You can use POPFile to separate your mail into personal and business mail or to separate messages that come from mailing lists or newsletters.

How POPFile classifies your messages

POPFile sorts your incoming messages into *buckets* (like folders) using several types of information to tag your e-mail messages. Unfortunately, POPFile uses its own, strange terms for this information:

Corpus: The collection of words that POPFile associates with a bucket. For example, the Spam bucket's corpus may include words like *debt* and *mortgage* and the names of various body parts not normally discussed in polite society. Surprisingly, POPFile looks only for individual words, not for phrases: the matching of phrases slows the process too much.

Pseudowords: Nontext indicators telling POPFile that a message is likely to be spam. Spammers use various tricks to avoid getting detected as spam, such as bogus HTML codes and HTML comments within words,

words with spaces between each pair of letters, and messages that consist entirely of graphical images. POPFile looks for these tricks and figures that only spam would contain them!

Magnet: A word that, when it appears in a message header, tells POPFile to put the message in a specific bucket regardless of the other words in the message: It's a kind of override. For example, you may want your boss's e-mail address to be a magnet for your Inbox bucket, to prevent any message from your boss from getting mixed in with the spam.

Armed with this information, POPFile uses Bayesian filtering to figure out which message goes in each of your buckets. (Refer to Chapter 1 to find out what the heck Bayesian filtering is.)

If you're using POPFile only to reduce the amount of spam you have to see, you need just two buckets: Spam and Inbox.

Installing POPFile

POPFile is an *open source* program, which means that you can download it and run it for free. The program's home page is at popfile.sourceforge.net — click English (or the language of your choice) to see instructions for downloading and installing the program.

POPFile comes in two versions:

- ✔ **Windows version:** This version is a ready-to-run version for Windows.

- ✔ **Perl version:** You may never have heard of Perl, but it's a widely used programming language, and Perl programs can run on the Mac and on Unix and Linux machines. Just make sure that you have Perl on your machine. See the POPFile manual (online at the POPFile site) for information.

Windows users can follow these steps:

1. **Download the Windows-ready version by starting at popfile.sourceforge.net/manual/installing. html and clicking the POPFile Download Page link. Select the latest version to download and store it on your hard disk.**

   You get a zip file (which Windows XP calls a compressed folder) with a name like popfile-v0.18.2-windows.zip.

2. **Open the zip file in Windows Explorer, by choosing My Computer, navigating to where you stored the file, and double-clicking the filename.**

   You see one file, setup.exe.

3. **Double-click the file to run the setup program.**

   A wizard runs and steps you through the installation. Click Next and Install to move from screen to screen.

   Among other things, the wizard offers you the option of *skins* (different color schemes for the POPFile windows) and languages (if you want to see the POPFile windows and prompts in a language other than English). Leave the POP3 port number set to 110 and the default port number for interface connections set to 8080, as the wizard suggests.

4. **Select the Run POPFile Automatically When Windows Starts check box so that POPFile is always ready to process your mail.**

5. **If the wizard finds Outlook Express on your machine (and because it comes with Windows, it does), it offers to set Outlook Express to get its mail via POPFile. Select the Reconfigure This Account To Work With POPFile check box if you use Outlook Express.**

   If you use another e-mail program, you need to configure it yourself, as described in the section "Configuring your e-mail program to work with POPFile ," later in this chapter. Don't worry about it now — just keep reading and following our instructions until you get to that section.

6. **Click Finish to close the wizard.**

7. **Start POPFile by choosing Start➪Programs➪ POPFile➪Run POPFile in the background.**

   Nothing appears to happen. But POPFile should be ready to scam for spam!

To ensure that POPFile is alive, Windows 2000 and Windows XP users can press Ctrl+Alt+Del to see the Windows Task Manager window and select the Processes tab. POPFile appears as Wperl.exe.

Setting POPFile to run on Windows Startup

Every time you start your computer and Windows, you need for POPFile to start too. Follow these steps to tell Windows to run POPFile in the background (that is, without a window) every time Windows starts (these instructions are for Windows XP):

1. **Choose Start⇨All Programs⇨POPFile.**

   You see a menu of installed POPFile programs.

2. **Find the Startup folder on the All Programs menu.**

   The programs in this folder run when Windows starts up.

3. **Click and drag the Run POPFile In Background option to the Startup folder. Don't release the mouse button yet.**

   A menu opens, showing the programs that now run on startup. (The menu may contain programs you didn't know about!)

4. **Move the mouse to that menu and release the mouse button to drop the POPFile entry into the Startup group.**

   Now POPFile runs whenever Windows runs.

Talking to POPFile

POPFile doesn't have its own window. Instead, to talk to POPFile, you use your Web browser. Run your browser and type this interesting-looking address:

```
127.0.0.1:8080
```

Yes, those are all numbers: 127.0.0.1 tells your browser to look on your own computer, and 8080 is the Internet port number on which POPFile communicates. Strange but true!

You see a Web page that looks like Figure 11-1: your POPFile Control Center. (This figure shows the page in the Netscape 7.1 browser, but the page itself looks about the same regardless of which browser you use.) If you have a version of POPFile later than 0.18.2, your Web page may look a little different.

In the POPFile Control Center, you create buckets to sort mail, correct POPFile when it sorts messages into the wrong bucket, and perform other configuration tasks.

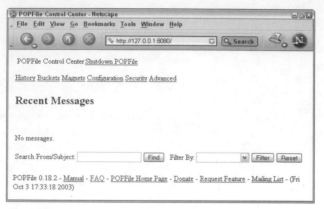

Figure 11-1: POPFile is ready to scan for spam.

Creating buckets in POPFile

After POPFile is up and running, you need to create a *bucket* for spam. Creating a bucket tells POPFile that you want messages tagged with [spam] on the Subject line (or a special X-Text-Classification header that includes the word *spam*) so that your e-mail program can filter these messages into the trash.

POPFile doesn't have to mess with your Subject lines

Normally, POPFile adds a bucket name to the beginning of the Subject line *and* adds an X-Text-Classification header line to each message. If your e-mail program can sort your incoming messages based on their header lines, you don't need for POPFile to mess with your Subject lines. To turn off Subject-line-messing, click the Configuration link in the POPFile Control Center, look in the E-Mail Text Insertion section of the page, and click the Turn Off button next to the label Subject Line Modification. This command turns off Subject line modification for all buckets.

Outlook and Eudora can filter all messages based on the X-Text-Classification (or any other) header. For details, see Part II.

To create a bucket for spam, follow these steps:

1. **Run your browser and go to this address:**

   `127.0.0.1:8080`

   You see the POPFile Control Center (refer to Figure 11-1).

2. **Click the Buckets link.**

   You see a summary of your buckets (as shown in Figure 11-2), with arcane statistics about them. Because you don't have any buckets yet, you don't see much.

3. **Scroll down to the Maintenance section, type** spam **in the Create Bucket With Name box, and click Create.**

   You have a bucket!

![POPFile Control Center window screenshot]

Figure 11-2: Make one bucket for spam and one for everything else.

We like to create two buckets: Spam and Inbox. We turn off Subject line modification for the Inbox bucket so that POPFile doesn't add [inbox] to the beginning of the Subject line of all our nonspam messages. To turn this feature off, go to the Buckets page in the POPFile Control Center and click the Turn Off button in the Subject Modification column, to the right of the Inbox bucket. You end up with a POPFile configuration that looks like Figure 11-2.

Now you can spot messages that POPFile thinks are spam because they have [spam] at the beginning of the Subject line.

Configuring your e-mail program to work with POPFile

If POPFile sees a copy of Outlook Express on your computer, it does part of the configuration for you. Otherwise, you need to make a note of how your program now gets the mail, tell the program to get messages from POPFile instead, and tell POPFile to use your e-mail program's settings to get your mail. The settings you need to note are shown in this list:

✔ **Incoming mail server:** The POP (or POP3) mail server that stores your incoming messages until you pick them up, usually provided by your ISP. You need to change this setting in your e-mail program from its current setting to 127.0.0.1, the address of POPFile running on your own computer.

✔ **User name:** The name your e-mail program uses to connect to your incoming mail server, almost always the same as the part of your e-mail address before the @. For example, if your address is billgates@microsoft.com, your user name is billgates. You need to change this name to a combination of your original incoming mail server name, a colon, and your user name. For example, if your incoming mail server is pop.earthlink.net, you may change this setting to pop.earthlink.net:billgates.

✔ **Password:** The password that your e-mail program uses to connect to your incoming mail server. Don't change this setting.

If you're not sure what your incoming mail server, user name, or password are, ask your ISP (assuming that you use the address your ISP provides with your account).

Even if you do use Outlook Express, you still need to tell it to direct any messages that POPFile has tagged as spam into your Suspected Spam or Deleted Items folder. Most e-mail programs let you create rules or filters for this purpose. (Part II contains detailed instructions for each major e-mail program.)

The following sections contain step-by-step instructions to configure your e-mail program to fetch your mail via POPFile rather than directly from your mail server, and to sort spam out of your inbox.

If you use Netscape 7.1, Mozilla 1.3, or Eudora 6, you already have spam-spotting features equivalent to POPFile's built in. Just turn them on! Refer to Chapters 7 and 8.

POPFile sometimes conflicts with virus checkers, firewalls, and other security software. If you run into trouble getting POPFile to work, read the online manual at

`popfile.sourceforge.net/manual/manual.html`

A FAQ (Frequently Asked Questions) file is also online: Go to `popfile.sourceforge.net`, clink the link for your language, and click the FAQ link. (It's toward the bottom of the page, last time we looked.)

Configuring Outlook Express or Outlook for POPFile

The POPFile installation program tries to set up Outlook Express for you, but you may want to double-check its settings. In Outlook Express or Outlook, follow these steps:

1. **Choose Tools⊃Accounts.**

   You see the Internet Accounts dialog box.

2. **Click the Mail tab.**

3. **Select your mail account if it's not already selected, and click the Properties button.**

   You see the Properties dialog box for your e-mail account.

4. **Click the Servers tab.**

   You see the dialog box shown in Figure 11-3.

5. **Change the Account Name setting from its current setting to your incoming mail server name, a colon, and your user name.**

   You can copy the server name from the Incoming Mail (POP3) setting.

6. **Change the Incoming Mail (POP3) setting from its current setting to** 127.0.0.1.

7. **Leave the rest of the settings alone, and click OK and then Close to save your changes.**

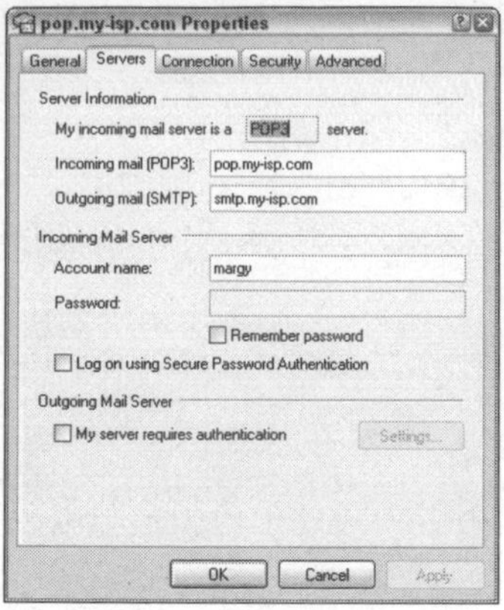

Figure 11-3: Changing your Outlook or Outlook Express configuration to use POPFile.

Outlook or Outlook Express now gets your mail via POPFile. Your other task is to create a rule that sorts your spam-tagged messages into the Deleted Items folder. See the section in Chapter 6 about creating rules to trash spam to find out how rules and filters can sort any messages with [spam] in them into the Deleted Items folder.

Outlook (but not Outlook Express) can sort messages based on the POPFile X-Text-Classification header, so you can avoid having the bucket name appear at the beginning of each message's Subject line. Follow the steps in the sidebar "POPFile doesn't have to mess with your Subject lines," earlier in this chapter. Then create a rule in Outlook that looks for messages that have this text in the header:

```
X-Text-Classification: spam
```

If you use Outlook, see the section in Chapter 6 about trapping spam based on the X-Text-Classification or other spam-tagging header.

Configuring Pegasus for POPFile

Pegasus (described in the Chapter 8 sidebar "Pegasus: An excellent, free e-mail program with built-in spam filtering") works with POPFile too. Follow these steps to configure Pegasus:

1. **Choose Files⇨Network Configuration or Tools⇨ Internet Options.**

   You see the Internet Mail Options dialog box.

2. **Click the Receiving (POP3) tab.**

3. **If a list of hosts appears, select your e-mail account and click Edit.**

4. **Change the User Name setting from its current setting to your incoming mail server name, a colon, and your user name.**

   You can copy the server name from the POP3 or Server Host Name setting.

5. **Change the POP3 host or Server host name from its current setting to** 127.0.0.1.

6. **Leave the rest of the settings alone and click OK to save your changes.**

Training POPFile

After POPFile is running and scanning all your incoming messages, you find that absolutely nothing happens! That's because it has no idea how to classify messages into buckets. You need tell it, by *training* it.

Giving POPFile the general idea

To train POPFile when you first start using it (it makes zillions of mistakes at first), follow these steps:

1. **In your e-mail program, give the command, click the button, press the keys, or otherwise cause the program to get your e-mail.**

   Your messages pass through POPFile on their way into your e-mail program. Later, you can read messages in the e-mail program and just use the POPFile Control Center to correct the occasional mistake. However, at the beginning, POPFile makes so many mistakes that it's easier to look at all your messages in the POPFile Control Center first.

2. **In another window, run your browser, bring up the POPFile page at** 127.0.0.1:8080, **and click the History link.**

You see a Web page that looks like the one shown in Figure 11-4.

3. **Look down the list of messages for messages that are misclassified or unclassified.**

   For each message, the history listing shows you the sender, the subject, the POPFile guess for the bucket, a drop-down box you can set to the correct bucket for the message, and a check box that lets you remove the message from the history list. At first, all messages are unclassified.

4. **For messages that aren't assigned to the right bucket (or that are unclassified), select the box in the Should Be column for the message and set it to the correct bucket. If you can't guess from the sender and the Subject line, click the Subject line to see the whole message.**

5. **Repeat Step 4 for all messages on the page.**

6. **When you get to the bottom of the page, click the Reclassify button to tell POPFile to update its bucket information.**

   POPFile redisplays the page, showing you where each message is now.

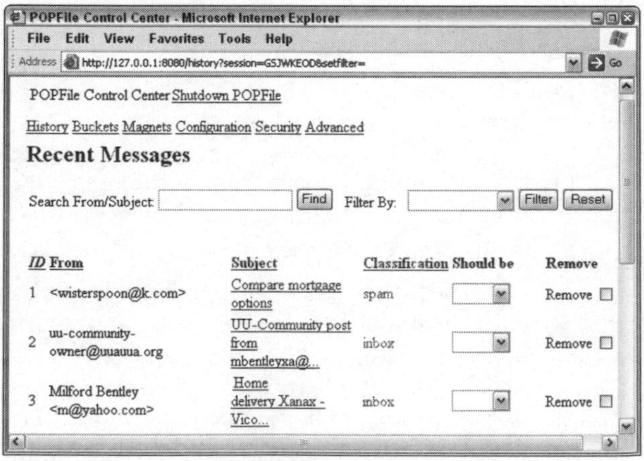

Figure 11-4: POPFile makes lots of mistakes until you train it to spot spam; click <u>History</u> to see how POPFile tagged your recent messages.

7. **To get rid of messages you have already fixed, click the Remove Page button.**

   POPFile displays the next page of messages, if you have more messages than fit on one page (POPFile usually displays 20 messages per page). Carry on, starting over at Step 3.

 If your e-mail program displays message headers, you can see the X-POPFile-Link header at the top of the message in your e-mail program, with a long, hairy-looking link, like this:

```
X-POPFile-Link:
<http://127.0.0.1:8080/jump_to_message?
view=popfile86=15.msg>
```

Click the link to jump directly to the POPFile Control Center page about that particular message. (The page appears in your browser window.)

Fixing the occasional POPFile mistake

After you have trained POPFile for a few days, the number of mistakes usually drops to just a few. Rather than look at the POPFile Control Center's History page first, you can switch to reading your e-mail as usual. Look through the messages in your Junk E-Mail or Suspected Spam folder (or wherever you're filtering your spam) for *false positives* — good messages that POPFile has erroneously mixed in with the junk. For each one, go to the POPFile Control Center's History page and find that message (or click its X-POPFile-Link header, if your e-mail program displays it). Reclassify the message from the Spam bucket to the Inbox bucket. Similarly, if POPFile misses any spam and it ends up in your inbox, reclassify it as spam.

Creating magnets for specific senders or text

If POPFile is having trouble guessing about some messages, you can overrule it by creating a *magnet* — a rule that POPFile applies before it starts using its own judgment about messages. For example, you may want to create magnets for the people from whom you hear most often, directing messages from these people into the Inbox folder regardless of their content. This type of magnet tells POPFile, "Don't bother looking inside these messages because, based on the sender, I want to read them no matter what." You can also create magnets for your Spam folder, indicating types of messages that are *always* spam.

To create a magnet, follow these steps:

1. **In your Web browser, go to the POPFile Control Center at** `http://127.0.0.1:8080` **and click the Magnets link.**

   You see a list of current magnets, which is empty unless you created some. POPFile doesn't create magnets on its own.

2. **Scroll down to the Creating New Magnet section and set the Magnet type to From (to specify by a sender's address), To (based on the addressee of the message), or Subject (based on the Subject line of the message).**

   For example, to say that *any* message that talks about debt reduction is spam, no matter what else it has in it, select Subject.

3. **In the Value box, type the address or text that you want POPFile to match.**

4. **Set the Always Goes To bucket box to the bucket where you want these messages to land.**

5. **Click the Create button.**

A disadvantage of using a stand-alone program like POPFile is that you can't just say "If a message is from an address in my e-mail program's address book, never put it in the Spam bucket." Programs with built-in spam checkers can provide this feature.

Adding Spam Bully to Outlook and Outlook Express

Spam Bully is an add-in for Outlook and Outlook Express that you can download from `www.spambully.com`. It's not free, but you can try it for free for a few weeks before deciding whether to buy it. Spam Bully uses a number of approaches to spam fighting, including

- ✔ Bayesian filtering (the method that POPFile uses).

- ✔ Bouncing messages back to spammers so that they think your address is no good (usually useless because most spammers don't care).

✔ Whitelisting your friends' addresses.

✔ Blacklisting spammer addresses.

✔ Sending challenge-response messages that reply to possible spam messages with a message to the sender, asking them to confirm with a password. (This technique stops spam, but annoys many real people who are trying to send you mail and often ignore the challenge.)

After you download the program file from the Spam Bully Web site, run the downloaded file to install it. Then, whenever you run Outlook Express or Outlook, it includes the Spam Bully add-in. The first time your e-mail program runs, Spam Bully needs to look at your existing mail configuration, including the mail messages that are already in your mail folders. When the program is done, you see a new toolbar in your e-mail program. (Figure 11-5 shows Spam Bully added to Outlook Express.)

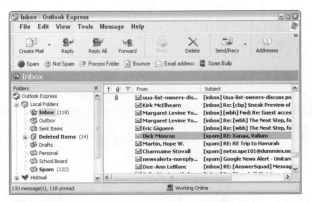

Figure 11-5: Spam Bully adds a toolbar to Outlook Express and Outlook.

Separating spam from mail with Spam Bully

The first time you get e-mail and Spam Bully gets to try out its filtering prowess, it creates a mail folder named Spam and moves spam messages there.

The first few times you get your e-mail, skim the messages in your Inbox and look for spam that Spam Bully missed. If you find any, click the Spam button on the new toolbar. Spam Bully moves the message to your Spam folder and learns not to miss that kind of message the next time.

Also, look at the messages in your Spam mailbox. At the beginning, Spam Bully may misidentify lots of good messages as spam. Select each one and click the Not Spam button.

To make Spam Bully take another look at messages in a mail folder, select the folder and click the Process Folder button on the toolbar. If your messages arrive from Hotmail or MSN or an IMAP or Exchange account, you may need to click this button each time mail arrives, to get spam out of your inbox.

If you have a folder that doesn't contain any spam, you can tell Spam Bully to learn from these messages. Open the folder, click the Spam Bully button on the toolbar, and choose Learn Folder As Regular Mail from the menu that appears.

Managing your black-and-white lists

Spam Bully maintains three lists of e-mail addresses for you:

- ✔ **Approved/Friends list:** Messages from this whitelist of addresses are never spam. Spam Bully adds addresses to this list whenever you use the Not Spam button to categorize messages.

- ✔ **Banned/Spammers list:** Messages from this blacklist of address are always considered to be spam.

- ✔ **Email addresses waiting to be approved:** These addresses have received a challenge e-mail from Spam Bully, but have not yet responded.

You can see and edit these lists by clicking the Email Address button on the Spam Bully toolbar.

Keeping Spam Bully under control

You can configure some Spam Bully settings by choosing Tools⇨Spam Bully Options. You see a dialog box with configuration settings, as shown in Figure 11-6.

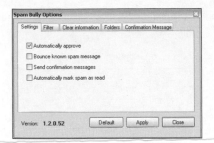

Figure 11-6: Configuring Spam Bully.

We don't recommend selecting the Bounce Known Spam Messages option because so many spammers forge their return addresses anyway. Don't select the Send Confirmation Messages check box either, unless you want to annoy your correspondents. Spam Bully should do an adequate job of cutting down on your spam without these measures.

If you want to see impressive-looking graphs of how much of your e-mail is spam, click the Spam Bully button on the toolbar and choose Statistics from the menu that appears.

Chapter 12

Antispam Services for Just Plain Folks

● ●

In This Chapter

▶ How spam-filtering services work

▶ Services that riffle through the messages in your existing mailbox

▶ Mail addresses that are filtered

▶ Mail addresses that are disposable

● ●

*Y*ou can depend on your ISP (Internet service provider) and the software on your own PC to deal with spam — that's the approach we talk about in the preceding chapters of this book. But we know another way, if you want to get serious about not getting any spam: You can subscribe to a variety of mail-filtering services.

Spam-filtering services fall into three general categories:

✔ Services that filter the mail inside your existing mailbox

✔ Services that provide a new address, filter mail sent to that address, and then either forward the result to your real address or let you pick it up with your e-mail program

✔ Services that let you create multiple addresses you can hand out to potentially untrustworthy correspondents and then discard addresses that get too much spam

Because most filtering services provide more than one kind of service, we list them together in the following sidebar, "Some spam-filtering services."

Some spam-filtering services

Here are a bunch of spam-filtering services to consider:

Cloudmark SpamNet, at www.cloudmark.com, is an add-in for Outlook and Outlook Express that filters spam by using a shared database of spam "fingerprints."

Despammed.com provides filtered e-mail, forwarded to your existing account or Web mail. It's free.

EMF Systems, at www.emailfiltering.co.uk (click the <u>Home Users</u> link), offers POP proxy filtering.

Myrealbox, at www.myrealbox.com, provides filtered mail with POP, IMAP, or Web mail. Myrealbox is offered for free by Novell, which uses it to test its NetMail product.

Pobox, at www.pobox.com, offers a variety of mail-forwarding services, including filtered addresses.

Spamcop, at www.spamcop.net, is mostly a spam-reporting service, and also offers filtered e-mail addresses.

Spamex, at www.spamex.com, provides disposable e-mail addresses.

Spamgourmet, at www.spamgourmet.com, provides self-destructing, disposable e-mail addresses. The service is free. It collects statistics on the mail that gets discarded.

Services that filter the mail in your existing mailbox work with your existing e-mail address. The other two kinds involve setting up a new address, or maybe lots of new addresses, at the filtering company. The multiple address services create addresses in addition to your regular address, so you may find them interesting even if you don't want to change your main e-mail address.

Some of these services are free, but most charge a monthly or annual fee. The paid services generally offer a way to try them out for free — a limited version, a free first month before they start charging, or a trial period during which you can cancel and get your money back.

Filters for Your Existing Mailbox

A few filtering services apply themselves to your existing mailbox. In some cases, the service acts as a *POP proxy,* which means that you give the service the login details for your e-mail mailbox (which must be stored on a POP server) and you get your mail via the service. It periodically picks up your mail, transfers it to its own system, and runs it through its filters. Then you pick up your nice, clean mail by either visiting the Web site or setting up your mail program to retrieve it from the service's POP server rather than from your ISP's.

Other filtering services provide a program that runs on your PC, like stand-alone filtering software, but connects to the service to get filter rules updates, checks whether particular messages match entries in their collections of known spam, and other tasks.

Here are some points to consider about this type of filtering service:

- If keeping the same e-mail address you already have is important, these services can supplant whatever filtering your main mail provider has without requiring you to get a new e-mail address.

- POP proxies delay your mail a little because you can't get your mail any faster than their system can pick it up from your original mailbox.

- Make sure that a service is trustworthy before you give it the keys to your real mailbox. (We haven't heard of any problems, but the possibility of trouble, either deliberate or accidental, is there.)

Filtered Mail Addresses

Many services offer *filtered* e-mail addresses, or mailboxes with spam-filtering built-in. You sign up for a filtered mail address the same way you sign up for a Web mail account like Hotmail or MSN or Yahoo! Mail, except that instead of (or in addition to) providing Web mail, the service either provides a POP server where you can pick up mail with your regular e-mail program or forwards the filtered mail to your existing e-mail address. Some services forward all your messages (spam and all), tagging the spam so that you can sort it in your mail program. Other services keep the spam on their servers so that you can check it over the Web, and others just throw the spam away.

Here's a good way to use a filtered mail address: If your existing address doesn't get much spam, keep using it and give that address only to friends and family. When you need to provide your e-mail address to anyone else, give the filtered mail address. This system does require that you check your messages in two e-mail accounts, but most e-mail programs handle multiple POP accounts. Be sure to choose a filtered mail service with a POP server, and then set up your e-mail program to collect your messages for both accounts. You can keep messages from your friends and family members separate from your filtered mail. Just be sure to use the right return address when you send mail!

Filter and fight spam at the same time at the SpamCon Foundation

The SpamCon Foundation is a donor-supported antispam organization run by friends of ours. On a shoe-string budget, it publishes a free newsletter, maintains online libraries of resources, and sponsors an occasional conference.

One way to support the foundation is to subscribe to its spam-filtering services. It offers Postini-filtered mail-boxes (as described in Chapter 13), ClicVU disposable e-mail addresses,

and more. The price is about the same as you would pay anywhere else, and you support SpamCon at the same time. Visit www.spamcon.org and click the Filtered or Disposable mail links on the left side of the home page. SpamCon lists, along with its own services, other mail-filtering services it knows about, so it's a good place to check regardless of whether you plan to use its filters.

If you use Outlook or Outlook Express for your mail program, you can use Hotmail or MSN as a filtered mail account because both programs can work directly with a Hotmail or MSN account. Or, if your favorite mail program is Netscape 7 or AOL Communicator, you can use an AOL account as your filtered mail address. (If that's your main use for AOL, you can switch to the $5-per-month plan. This plan includes only three hours of online time, but because sending and receiving mail through Netscape or Communicator don't count as online time, three hours is plenty.)

Lots of Mail Addresses

Disposable e-mail addresses let you give different addresses to each potentially untrustworthy correspondent. Every time you order stuff from a new store online, you can give the vendor a new e-mail address. All the addresses land in the same mailbox; either they arrive in a POP mailbox provided by the filtering service or they're forwarded to your regular address. For example, you may give the address elvis-123@example.com when you buy items from a bookstore and elvis-456@example.com when you buy caviar (as you often do, we're sure). Mail to both these addresses lands in your elvis@example.com mailbox.

If you find that one of your disposable addresses starts getting more spam than you want, you just turn that address off. John has long done something similar (he runs his own mail server, which made it easy to set up): He gives a unique address each time he has to provide one when ordering something online or otherwise giving an address to someone new. Although he has found that he hasn't needed to dispose of many of them, it's still often handy to see which address a dubious piece of mail was sent to, and usually to say "Ah, now I remember — I gave them that address."

Your ISP may provide something like disposable addresses automatically. Most ISPs let you set up anywhere from five to eight addresses per account, and they let you throw away an address and set up a new one as often as you want. You can also often use subaddresses, such as fred-xyz@myisp.com

or `fred+xyz@myisp.com` if your address is `fred@myisp.com`.
Check with your ISP; in many cases the ISP's mail system han-
dles subaddresses automatically. You can't turn them off, but
you can usually arrange to filter mail based on the subaddress
in your mail program. (See Part II of this book to find out how
to filter or sort mail in your e-mail program.)

Chapter 13

Server-Side Spam Filtering for Network Administrators

*1*f you run a mail server, you should run spam-filtering software for the benefit of your users. Server-side filtering has both technical and, shall we say, social advantages:

✔ Server filters can do a better job than user filters (filters on the user's computer) because the server has access to the entire stream of incoming mail.

✔ Spam and virus filtering can often be done at the same time.

✔ If the filters reject mail or divert mail into a separate mailbox on the server, users don't have to download mail that they're only going to throw away.

✔ Users don't have to install their own filtering software.

✔ You don't have to try to support 17 different random filtering programs that users download off the Net.

Server Filtering Techniques

In Chapter 1, we mention three general filtering techniques: whitelists, blacklists, and message filters. When you run the filter on your mail server, some techniques become practical that aren't when they're applied individually by users. A server filter should be able to use these techniques, individually or in combination:

- ✔ **IP address filtering:** The filter tests the numeric IP address from which the mail arrives, to reject mail from known problem addresses. Most filters let you set IP address ranges to blacklist or whitelist directly, but using shared blacklists and whitelists distributed via the Net's Domain Name System (DNS) is much more common.

- ✔ **Bulk counting:** The essence of spam is that a whole lot of it is out there. Bulk counting filters look at incoming mail to try to recognize when many similar messages are arriving.

- ✔ **Timing techniques and greylists:** Filters can often detect spam by looking at peculiarities of the rate at which it arrives.

- ✔ **Body filters:** These filters look at the contents of the spam, just like desktop filters do. Because the server filter can see all incoming mail, not just one user's, Bayesian and other adaptive techniques can use a larger sample base.

The next three sections explore these types of filtering in more detail.

DNS blacklists and whitelists

One of the most effective server filtering techniques is to reject mail based on its sending IP address. Because the IP address is known at the beginning of the incoming mail connection, a server can use IP rejection to refuse even to receive a message, which is much faster than receiving and then discarding mail. Conversely, if a message is coming from an IP that's known to send no spam, the mail system can bypass the rest of the filters.

The standard way to distribute shared lists of IP addresses is a *DNSBL* (*DNS–based list*). The original DNSBL was Paul Vixie's Realtime Blackhole List (RBL), but now hundreds of DNSBLs are out there, ranging from widely used professional lists to tiny, sloppily run personal lists.

DNSBLs work by making up a domain name for every possible IP address. If the address you want to check is 169.254.100.5 and the DNSBL is spam.services.net, the filter reverses the order of the components in the IP address and looks up this address in the DNS system:

```
5.100.254.169.spam.services.net
```

If that name exists in the DNS entry, the address is in the DNSBL. (The reverse order makes it easier for a DNSBL to handle ranges of addresses.)

Because DNS lookups are quite fast, filters can use DNSBLs to check the IP address of each incoming mail message at the moment the sending system connects to the mail server.

Popular DNSBLs include the ones in this list:

✔ **Spamhaus Block List (SBL),** at www.spamhaus.org/sbl: The most widely used DNSBL in the world; lists verified high-volume spam sources. It blocks lots of spam sent by professional spammers.

✔ **Composite Blocking List (CBL),** at cbl.abuseat.org: An automatically maintained list of sources of verified spam. This list blocks lots of spam sent through open proxies and other hijacked machines.

✔ **Relay Stop List (RSL),** at relays.visi.com: An automatically maintained list of verified, insecure open relays with a history of sending spam.

✔ **Open Relay DataBase (ORDB),** at www.ordb.org: Another open relay list, more aggressive than RSL.

✔ **Not Just Another Bogus List (NJABL),** at njabl.org: A combination list of open relays, proxies, dial-ups, and spam sources. It's more aggressive than RSL and ORDB, but still fairly reliable.

✔ **Easynet lists** at `abuse.easynet.nl`: DNSBLs of spam sources, insecure open proxies, and dial-up and similar dynamically assigned addresses that shouldn't be sending mail directly, maintained by a large ISP in the Netherlands.

✔ **SpamCop Blocking List,** at `spamcop.net/bl.shtml`: An aggressive list of spam sources driven by user reports. This list blocks a great deal of spam, but because it has a much higher error rate than other DNSBLs in this list, it's useful only as a component of a scoring filter.

✔ **MAPS RBL PLUS** and related lists from `www.mail-abuse.org`: The descendant of the original RBL; includes the RBL (spam sources), DUL (dial-up and dynamic address ranges), RSS (open relays), and OPL (open proxies). These lists require a license from MAPS to use, and their prices range from $0 for small private networks to $10,000 per year for large corporations and ISPs.

Bulk counting

One of the most effective approaches to recognizing spam on a server is bulk counting. Each time a message arrives, the filter makes a *hash* (compressed) code representing the contents of the message and looks in a database to see how many other messages have arrived recently with the same hash code. If it's several, the message is probably spam. Because spammers tend to mutate their messages to avoid bulk counting filters, effective bulk counters also make "fuzzy" hash codes designed to disregard minor differences between one copy of a message and another. Bulk counters recognize bulk mail from legitimate mailing lists as well as spam, so any bulk counting system needs to be configured to whitelist known legitimate mail, usually based on the return address, the sending IP, and a whitelist of the hash codes of mailing list messages.

Bulk counting doesn't need to be restricted to a single mail server. The best bulk counting systems exchange hash code information among many servers.

The premier bulk counting system is the Distributed Checksum Clearinghouse, at `www.dcc-servers.net`, which coordinates a network of more than 150 servers that check more than 50 million messages a day. Although networks that handle small amounts of mail (fewer than about 50,000 messages a day) are welcome to use the public DCC servers, larger mail users should arrange to run their own DCC server.

Timing and greylists

Most spam is sent by specialized *spamware* that blasts out mail as fast as possible without checking for errors rather than by normal mail software. Viruses and worms often skip the error checking too. Spamware and viruses frequently can be detected by looking for timing peculiarities caused by the lack of error checking.

The mail server and the sending host normally exchange messages in lockstep, with the sending host sending a command, the server replying with a status message, the sending host sending another command, and so on. Because the sequence of commands and status messages is completely predictable for successful message delivery, spamware often sends all the commands without waiting for the replies. The server can check to see whether the sending computer is getting ahead of the replies, and if so, reliably conclude that the mail is coming from spamware or a virus rather than from a real mail client.

Another timing trick available to servers is *greylisting*. If a mail server is short of disk space or is otherwise suffering from problems that temporarily keep it from receiving mail, it can return `temporary error` status codes to attempts to send it mail. Real mail programs retry the message a little later, but viruses and spamware don't bother. The idea of greylisting is that when a server sees an incoming message from a hitherto unknown server, the server returns a temporary error message and remembers the sender's IP address along with the sender and recipient addresses of the temporarily rejected message. If the sender retries the same message reasonably soon — recognized by the same IP, sender, and recipient — the server accepts it and also accepts future mail from that IP without delays. If not, the server continues to send temporary rejections to mail from that IP. Experiments show that this process delays about 4 percent of legitimate mail for an hour or so (most mail comes from IP addresses that have sent mail before) while rejecting nearly all mail sent by spamware.

Both these tricks have to be implemented in mail server software because only the server knows the timing of incoming mail. Greylisting is not yet widely used, but the DCC software can be configured to do greylisting as well as bulk counting.

Approaches to Combination Filtering

For spam filters that use multiple tests (all the effective ones), you have two different ways to handle the multiple tests: sequentially or by scoring.

- Some filters apply tests *sequentially,* typically doing their IP tests first as the remote host connects and then their bulk tests and then their body tests. If any of the tests categorizes a message as spam, the filter stops and doesn't do any more testing on that message.

- *Scoring* filters, on the other hand, run all their tests, assign a weight to each test, and add (or otherwise average) the weights of the tests that the message passed. If the score is above a threshold level, the message is considered to be spam. (See the section "Filtering on Unix and Linux Servers," later in this chapter, for an example of scoring using SpamAssassin.)

Sequential filters can be much faster because they often don't need to run the full set of tests, but they're harder to tune than scoring filters. A hybrid approach is often most effective. On our mail servers, we test at connection-time some conservative DNSBLs with low false positive rates (currently SBL, CBL, Easynet, MAPS, and a private local list) and reject any addresses they list. Then we use SpamAssassin on the mail we do accept for its scoring filters. The connection-time filters reject between 40 percent and 50 percent of incoming mail attempts, with a corresponding drop in the amount of mail that SpamAssassin has to handle.

If You Use Windows Server and Exchange

Starting from a weak base, Microsoft has improved the security of its Exchange mail server in each version so that Exchange 2003, along with the SMTP server in recent versions of the IIS Web server, can be configured to be fairly secure. Neither Exchange nor IIS includes built-in spam filtering, but they have provisions for plug-in filters.

Dozens of vendors offer filtering software, most of which combines spam filtering with virus filtering, which on a Windows system is at least as essential as spam filtering. Some filtering products arc shown in this list:

- ✔ Brightmail (www.brightmail.com); see the section "But, Does It Make Toast?" later in this chapter.

- ✔ GFI Mail Essentials (www.gfisoftware.com).

- ✔ Hexamail Guard (www.hexamail.com).

- ✔ MailMarshal (www.mailmarshal.com).

- ✔ Mail Storage Guard (www.mapilab.com).

- ✔ Symantec AntiVirus for SMTP Gateways (www.symantec.com).

Different versions of Exchange (versions 5.5 to 2003), as well as Lotus Domino and other groupware packages, require different versions of antispam and antivirus packages. Visit the vendors' Web sites to see whether they support the version you're using.

Microsoft Exchange isn't the only mail server available for Windows. More secure alternatives support the Outlook calendar and groupware features while providing better e-mail handling and filtering. Take a look at Communigate Pro, from Stalker Software, at www.stalker.com.

Filtering on Unix and Linux Servers

Internet e-mail grew up on Unix servers, so it's not surprising that a wide variety of both e-mail software and filtering add-ons are available for Unix and Linux. Nearly all of them are open source or freeware.

The most widely used Unix/Linux mail server is the venerable sendmail program, which has been around for more than 20 years. Not surprisingly, it has provisions to plug in many sorts of mail filters, with direct support for DNSBLs and a *milter* (*m*ail *filter*) framework to run other sorts of filters as mail is received. Other popular mail servers (including exim, postfix, and qmail) also support DNSBLs and have varying degrees of support for receipt-time filtering.

Unix/Linux mail systems usually also use procmail, a popular filtering package that runs as mail is being delivered to local mailboxes. Procmail has its own pattern-matching language that has been used to write filters such as Spambouncer (available at www.spambouncer.org), and it can run other programs, the usual way to run other filters.

By far the most popular Unix/Linux filter is SpamAssassin, at spamassassin.org. This effective scoring filter can use DNSBLs, DCC, and Razor (another shared hash counting system), along with fixed, heuristic, and Bayesian filters. SpamAssassin runs each message through all the tests it's configured to use, computes a *spamminess* score, and adds a report to the message header. Here's a full-detail report for a typical piece of spam that SpamAssassin caught:

```
X-Spam-Level: ************************
X-Spam-Checker-Version: SpamAssassin 2.60
(1.212-2003-09-23-exp) on
   tom.iecc.com
X-Spam-Flag: YES
X-Spam-Report:
   * 2.7 MIME_BOUND_RKFINDY Spam tool pattern in
MIME boundary (rfkindy)
   * 1.3 X_PRIORITY_HIGH Sent with 'X-Priority'
set to high
   * 0.3 FROM_HAS_MIXED_NUMS From: contains
numbers mixed in with letters
```

```
   *   1.6 X_LIBRARY Message has X-Library header
   *   0.1 HTML_70_80 BODY: Message is 70% to 80%
HTML
   *   0.1 HTML_FONTCOLOR_BLUE BODY: HTML font
color is blue
   *   1.2 MIME_HTML_MOSTLY BODY: Multipart message
mostly text/html MIME
   *   5.4 BAYES_99 BODY: Bayesian spam probability
is 99 to 100%
   *        [score: 1.0000]
   *   0.1 HTML_MESSAGE BODY: HTML included in
message
   *   1.5 HTTP_ESCAPED_HOST URI: Uses %-escapes
inside a URL's hostname
   *   0.8 HTTP_EXCESSIVE_ESCAPES URI: Completely
unnecessary %-escapes inside a URL
   *   2.5 FORGED_HOTMAIL_RCVD2 hotmail.com 'From'
address, but no 'Received:'
   *   4.1 HEAD_ILLEGAL_CHARS Header contains too
many raw illegal characters
   *   2.6 FORGED_MUA_OUTLOOK Forged mail
pretending to be from MS Outlook
   *   0.5 MIME_BOUND_NEXTPART Spam tool pattern in
MIME boundary
X-Spam-Status: Yes, hits=24.7 required=6.0
tests=BAYES_99,

FORGED_HOTMAIL_RCVD2,FORGED_MUA_OUTLOOK,FROM_HAS_
MIXED_NUMS,

HEAD_ILLEGAL_CHARS,HTML_70_80,HTML_FONTCOLOR_BLUE
,HTML_MESSAGE,

HTTP_ESCAPED_HOST,HTTP_EXCESSIVE ESCAPES,MIME_BOU
ND_NEXTPART,

MIME_BOUND_RKFINDY,MIME_HTML_MOSTLY,X_LIBRARY,X_P
RIORITY_HIGH
   autolearn=spam version=2.60
```

Our copy of SpamAssassin is set up to tag as spam anything that scores higher than 6.0; this message scored 24.7, which is extremely high. (Into the trash with it!)

SpamAssassin is most often run from procmail when mail is delivered, and less often as mail is received. Regardless of when SpamAssassin runs, it adds its report and usually marks the Subject line of tagged messages with *****SPAM*****. System managers — and in some cases, users — can easily configure the mail system to deliver tagged spam to a separate mailbox or even to discard it.

Quite a bit of other antispam software is available for Unix/Linux, most of which works in conjunction with SpamAssassin:

- ✔ **DCC,** from www.dcc-servers.net: Client and server software for the DCC bulk counting system. This program can be used via a sendmail milter, at delivery time from procmail, or from SpamAssassin.

- ✔ **amavisd-new,** from www.ijs.si/software/amavisd: A package that runs spam and virus filters from mail servers. Amavisd-new can call both SpamAssassin and an antivirus package, such as Clamav, from sendmail and other mail servers. (The original amavis is just a virus-scanning framework without spam filtering.)

- ✔ **Vipul's Razor,** from razor.sourceforge.net: A collaborative spam-filtering system, sort of like DCC. Rather than perform pure bulk counting, Razor accepts user submissions of spam and maintains a database of hash codes of reported spam. It's now usually used via SpamAssassin or the commercial Cloudmark service.

- ✔ **Maia Mailguard,** at www.renaissoft.com/projects/maia: A Web console for amavisd-new that lets users adjust the way their mail is filtered.

But, Does It Make Toast?

Because spam filtering is a complex and CPU-intensive application, you may want to consider dedicating a separate server to it. Many vendors offer antispam *appliances* already configured with antispam software that logically sits between the Internet and the existing mail server. The network mail configuration is adjusted so that incoming mail goes to the appliance, which examines the mail and remails the filtered mail to the existing mail server. Some appliances are physically installed next to the mail servers they support, and others sit at the vendor's site, passing filtered mail over the Internet.

Many vendors sell appliances containing versions of SpamAssassin, amavisd, DCC, Linux or other freeware Unix, and other freeware antispam software. We suggest that if that's the software you want, you're better off taking an old PC and hiring someone knowledgeable to set it up with filtering software so that you know what you have.

Spam-filtering appliances with software beyond what's available for free are sold by Network Associates, Symantec, Computer Associates, and a plethora of smaller companies.

Third-Party Services

Some vendors that offer software and services beyond the familiar freeware offerings are described in this list:

- ✓ **Brightmail,** at brightmail.com: Provides a subscription-filtering system that uses continually updated filter rules maintained by the Brightmail staff. Available as an appliance or as an Exchange add-on, it's used by several big ISPs and corporations that can afford the extra hardware it can sometimes require.

- ✓ **Postini,** at www.postini.com: Offers a filtering service. Incoming mail is routed to the Postini servers, which then forward the filtered mail to the customer's mail system. Postini is a popular choice of many small ISPs that don't mind outsourcing a key service like e-mail.

- ✓ **Spam Squelcher,** at spamsquelcher.com: Serves as a traffic-shaping appliance rather than a spam filter. Functioning like a network router, it sits at the edge of your network and passes all the data through to your servers. But when it sees network paths that are sending you spam, it uses a feature of the Transmission Control Protocol (the TCP in TCP/IP) to control, or *squelch,* the rate at which data packets can leave the spammer's computer. Although it passes all incoming mail through to the mail server eventually, good mail gets through faster. Because spamware tends to give up if mail is delayed, delayed spam tends to disappear and any misidentified real mail eventually gets through. On the downside, SpamSquelcher is appropriate only for ISPs and enterprises with more than a few thousand e-mail users.

A Checklist for Server Spam Filters

No matter what kind of server spam filter you decide on, make sure that it offers all these features:

- ✓ Regular updates to handle improvements in spam recognition and the latest spammer tricks

- ✓ Multiple filtering techniques, including IP-based, fixed body filters, adaptive (Bayesian) body filters, bulk counting, and greylists

- ✓ System-wide and per-user configuration to deal with individual preferences, false positives, and new spam variants

Part IV
The Part of Tens

The 5th Wave   By Rich Tennant

"TELL THE BOSS HE'S GOT MORE FLAME MAIL FROM YOU-KNOW-WHO."

In this part . . .

No *For Dummies* book is complete without "The Part of Tens." Here, you'll find two useful collections of information: a list of spam-based scams to avoid (or to make fun of your friends for believing) and our top ten Internet annoyances and what to do about them.

Chapter 14

Ten Spam Scams

● ●

In This Chapter

▶ Lose money in lots of different ways!

▶ Poison yourself!

▶ Persuade your friends that you're a sucker!

● ●

*O*ne of the few things you can count on when you get spammed is that whatever it claims to be offering, it's not for real. Herewith, we offer some of the greatest hits in spam scams.

Help Steal Millions from an African Country

Probably the best-developed spam scam is the 419 scam, named after the section of Nigerian law that makes it illegal. You receive an urgent message, most often from Nigeria, but sometimes from other countries in Africa or occasionally elsewhere. Your correspondent urgently needs your help to spirit away millions of dollars that are tied up in an account belonging to a deceased general or a crooked official at the national oil company. You will be well rewarded with a large percentage of the take.

What's going on? Well, before you can get your hands on the loot, a few details need to be worked out, officials need to be bribed, marker dye must be washed off the cash, and you need to send only a small advance to get things going. As we hope should be obvious, the millions are a fantasy, and if you're so foolish as to send the advance, that's the last you ever see of your money. What's astonishing is that people fall for this scam all the time, with individual losses up to hundreds of thousands of dollars and a total annual take in the billions, making it one of the largest industries in Nigeria. People occasionally go to Nigeria to try to recover their money. The lucky ones come back broke but alive. Some don't come back at all.

Although this *advance fee* scam has been perfected in the modern era in Nigeria, in its earlier form it was known as the Spanish prisoner, with the story that a rich nobleman was in prison in Spain and if you would front the money to bribe his way home, he would repay you tenfold *and* his beautiful daughter would show her appreciation, if you know what we mean. (For suckers with morals, an alternative version promised her hand in marriage.) This scam has been traced back to the 1500s, telling us that neither greed, nor gullibility, is a recent invention.

Make Lots of Money with No Work

Just call this toll-free number and you're on the road to riches. Or, more likely, to the poorhouse. The Federal Trade Commission says that these scams usually turn out to be illegal pyramid schemes, a well-known and completely illegal type of scam. The nature of pyramid schemes is to vacuum money upward from the suckers at the bottom of the pyramid toward the crooks at the top who started it. Needless to say, you start at the bottom.

Other versions are envelope-stuffing schemes (where the envelopes you stuff are full of more ads to even more suckers offering to sell them the same envelope-stuffing scam) or spam telling you that you can make tons of money if you buy the spammer's guaranteed path to riches by sending even more spam (which, of course, is the same spam you're supposed to sell to another generation of suckers).

You've Won a Free Vacation

Wow, you've won a free vacation to Disney World or the Bahamas! Let's go! Well, you may have to pay a modest charge for postage and handling, only slightly more than what the plane tickets would normally cost. And the hotel is a dump, if it even exists, and before you can check in, you have to sit through a high-pressure time-share sales presentation. And rooms are available only on Tuesdays and Wednesdays in November.

You can certainly find reasonably priced vacation packages to Florida and other places, but you find them on reputable travel Web sites, like Orbitz and Travelocity or on the travel pages of your local paper, not in spam.

Verify Your Account — Not!

Your ISP sends you an e-mail message saying that it's having a problem with your credit card, so for verification purposes please fill out a form with your account name, password, address, card number, and expiration date. Or, maybe the message comes from a familiar commerce site, like eBay or Amazon.com.

Real ISPs and Web sites never, *ever,* send mail like this. In the unlikely event that one of them has a problem with your credit card, someone there may send you a paper letter and ask you to call. The spam, some of which uses extremely authentic-looking graphics (swiped from the real Web site, natch!), sends your info back to the spammer, who then verifies your credit card by buying a whole bunch of stuff and charging it to you.

This scam — pretending to be someone with whom you do business to steal your account info or credit card details — is known to aficionados as *phishing*. Don't take the bait.

Get Free Cable or Satellite TV

Who wants to pay $40 every month for cable TV and even more for premium channels? When you get spam offering to sell you plans for a cable descrambler or the descrambler itself, is this an opportunity to $ave big buck$? Of course not, for the obvious reason that it doesn't work. A long, long time ago, some cable systems used simple scrambling schemes that could be defeated by gizmos built from parts bought at Radio Shack, but unless your cable box dates from about 1975, they don't work any more.

One thing you may be looking forward to is a visit from the cops. Stealing cable TV service is illegal, and if your cable company can detect that you're trying to do it, it isn't amused.

Repair Your Bad Credit

This scam comes in a variety of versions: Clean up your credit report or get a brand-new credit report, get a guaranteed credit card, or otherwise cast aside the burden of bad debt. In its simplest form, you pay someone to do the whammy on your credit report and that person takes your money and disappears. (Simple and elegant, isn't it?) Or, someone may tell you to get a business ID number from the IRS and use that number rather than your Social Security number to apply for credit, a clever idea that fools credit issuers and credit bureaus for, oh, the better part of three seconds. (Someone has already tried it? Gosh, what a surprise.)

The credit card may be a secured card for which you pay a $500 cash deposit and get a card with a high annual fee, a higher interest rate, and a $350 credit limit, which kind of stretches the definition of credit. Or, someone offers you a "gold card," good only for buying overpriced junk from their own catalog.

If you have credit problems, your best bet is probably to get from the library a book that tells you how to make a budget and work out payment plans with creditors. Or, you may have a reputable nonprofit credit counseling organization in your community. But fix your credit via spam? We don't think so.

Become Thin and Beautiful

Lose weight, grow more hair in desirable places, erase your zits, and otherwise become just like all those thin and beautiful people you see on TV by taking our guaranteed herbal nostrums.

You have already guessed: They don't work. The only thing we can guarantee is that if you send them your money, it's gone.

Get Drugs Without a Prescription, Cheap

This scam is the brand-name variant of the one in the preceding section. Need Vicodin, Vioxx, Propecia, human growth hormone, or (how did humankind ever live without it?) Viagra? No problem — we have whatever you need. No prescription? No problem! We have unethical doctors who can write you a prescription sight unseen, or we can just skip that step and ship it to you, maybe from our Canadian supplier or from a shipment that fell off a truck in Pakistan, or we may just compress talcum powder into pill shapes.

What's the hitch? Surely you don't think that if you send these guys money, they send you real prescription drugs that normally cost anywhere from $10 to $100 a dose, even in foreign countries. What can you do if they don't? You can hardly call the cops and complain, "I sent them money to buy drugs illegally without a prescription, but all they sent me was a bottle full of wood shavings from a hamster cage"?

For people who need the same prescription filled every month, legitimate mail-order pharmacies indeed have good prices. But they don't advertise with spam.

Make, Uh, Your Body Parts Bigger

You know what we mean. (In the unlikely event that you don't, refer to the fake Viagra in the preceding section and use your imagination.) For any individual spam, you have about a 50 percent chance of even having the part it's offering to expand; if you do, the nostrums range from exercises to herbal potions to stick-on patches. (Ouch!)

One report we read said that a journalist bought a bunch of different enlargement nostrums from a spammer, had them analyzed, and despite the fact that their alleged purposes and effects were quite different, they were all the same stuff. The main active ingredient that was found was *E. coli* bacteria, a hint that perhaps the manufacturers should have washed their hands before they started mixing.

This scam is amazingly successful. At a meeting of state attorneys general that Ray attended, the Arizona attorney general's office reported that it had recovered about $30 million from enlargement scammers and was prepared to refund it to dissatisfied customers. Few requests were received, presumably because not many people are prepared to say "My, um, you know, is still too small, and I'm really gullible."

Free Porn

Porn spam often says that it's free, free, FREE! Get all the porn you want for FREE! Click here and you're on your way.

Wait! We wouldn't want to expose any innocent children to our heavy breathing, even though the spam itself already exposed quite a bit. To make sure that you're a mature adult over 21, we just need to verify your credit card number. Don't worry — even though we have your name, address, and credit card number, we would never dream of charging anything to your card. Yeah, right.

A variation requires you to download a free "viewer" program. What you don't know is that this viewer program causes your computer to dial in to the Internet via an international long-distance number at exorbitant rates.

Chapter 15

Ten Internet Annoyances and How to Get Rid of Them

• •

In This Chapter

▶ Stop browser windows from popping up

▶ Put a firewall between you and the Internet

▶ Install a virus checker

▶ Remove adware and spyware from your computer

▶ Display lots of Web pages at the same time

▶ Erase your browsing history

▶ Find pagesseem to have vanished

▶ Reload Web pages

▶ Send e-mail to a list of friends

• •

*M*ost Internet users feel that spam is the bane of their Internet experience — some people have even quit using e-mail because of spam. The level of unpleasantness that spam injects into the Internet experience is just too high to be worth it for them.

However, spam is far from the only annoyance about the Internet. This chapter lists some other pain-in-the-neck aspects of the Internet and ways to avoid them. If you have your spam problem under control, why put up with browser pop-ups, viruses, adware, and other annoyances?

Squashing Browser Pop-Ups

Years ago, some clever Web programmer invented a way for a Web page to open additional browser windows. It wasn't a bad invention at first because, sometimes, working with several browser windows at the same time is convenient. However, marketing slimeballs have seized on the idea, and new windows now pop up continually, usually with annoying ads.

You have two ways to deal with browser pop-ups:

- ✔ Use a browser that blocks pop-ups.
- ✔ Install a pop-up blocker utility.

Netscape Navigator 7 and Mozilla can block pop-ups themselves. Choose Edit➪Preferences, double-click the Privacy & Security category to open it (unless its subcategories are already visible), and select the Popup Windows category, as shown in Figure 15-1. Select the Block Unrequested Popup Windows check box (it's selected by default). If you want to allow pop-ups from specific sites (for example, if an online game you enjoy uses pop-ups), click the Allowed Sites button and add the address of the Web site. AOL users have a pop-up blocker button at the bottom of their browser windows.

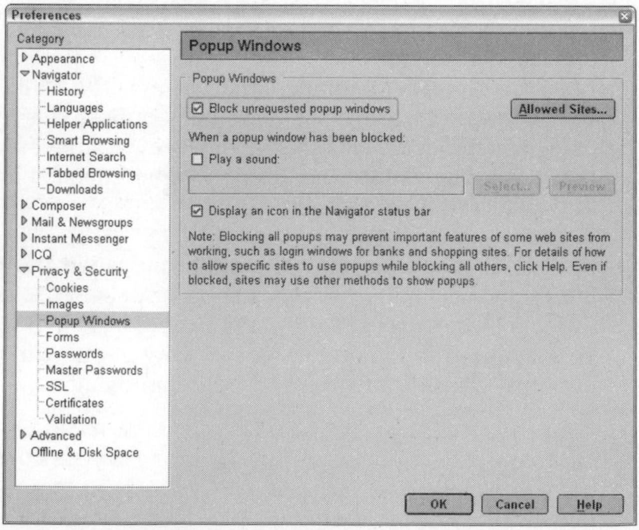

Figure 15-1: Netscape 7 and Mozilla have built-in pop-up stoppers.

If you insist on using Internet Explorer, many third-party pop-up stoppers are available. Many are free, or you can pay good money for programs that are no better than the free ones. We like the Google toolbar, which you can download from `toolbar.google.com`. The Google toolbar appears in Internet Explorer just below the Address box, with a box for Google-searching the Web directly from the toolbar. It also adds pop-up blocking and form-fill-ins to your browser. The Blocked button on the toolbar (shown in Figure 15-2 as `2 blocked`) indicates how many pop-ups Google has blocked for this Web site. To allow pop-ups from a site, click the button.

| Google▼ | | ▼ | Search Web ▼ | | PageRank | 2 blocked | AutoFill | | Options |

Figure 15-2: The Google toolbar.

Some other pop-up stoppers to consider are the shareware programs CoffeCup PopUp Blocker (`www.coffeecup.com/software`), Pop-Up Stopper (`www.panicware.com`), and STOPzilla (`www.stopzilla.com`).

And now, a word from our lawyer, who in this case is also our co-author, Ray: Yes, pop-up ads on Web sites can be annoying, but when you choose to block those advertisements, you're cutting into the method by which that Web site pays its bills. Some Web sites let you do away with annoying advertising, for a price. So, before you go blocking the occasional annoying ad, ask yourself how much you would pay to access that same site. If everybody blocks ads and the site earns no advertising revenue, you may end up asking that question for real. *Remember:* If your computer is infected with adware or spyware, the pop-up ads you see all the time may not even be the fault of the Web site you're visiting. Shutting them down may make the legitimate pop-up ads far less frequent and much less annoying.

Protecting Your System from Intruders

A *firewall* controls what kinds of information can pass between your computer and the rest of the world. If your computer connects directly to the Internet (rather than to a local-area network, or LAN, that connects to the Internet), you need a firewall between you and the Net.

Windows XP comes with the Internet Connection Firewall. If you use the New Connection Wizard to set up your Internet connection, you can turn it on; in fact, the firewall is on by default. Here's how to check whether it's on and turn it on if it's off:

1. **Choose Start⇨Control Panel⇨Network And Internet Connections⇨Network Connections.**

   You see the Network Connections window. Your Internet connection should appear in the Dial-Up or LAN or High-Speed Internet sections of the window.

2. **Right-click to select your Internet connection and choose Properties from the menu that appears.**

3. **Select the Advanced tab on the Properties dialog box, as shown in Figure 15-3.**

   The tab contains two sections: Internet Connection Firewall and Internet Connection Sharing.

4. **If the check box labeled "Protect My Computer And Network By Limiting Or Preventing Access To This Computer From The Internet isn't selected, click to select it.**

   That's all there is to it — you have no settings to configure.

5. **Click OK.**

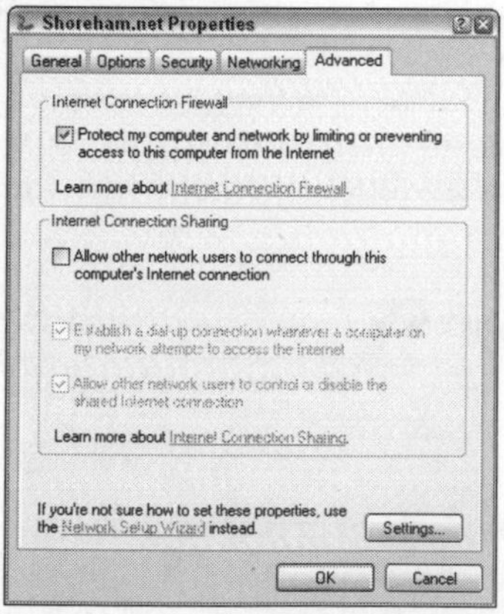

Figure 15-3: Turning on the Internet Connection Firewall in Windows XP.

If your computer is on a LAN, don't turn on the Internet Connection Firewall, which blocks file- and printer-sharing on the LAN.

Don't Let Viruses In

Anyone who doesn't run a virus checker on an Internet-connected computer is just asking for trouble. To find out everything you ever wanted to know about fighting back against viruses, pick up a copy of *Internet Privacy For Dummies*, written by two of the authors of this book (and published by Wiley Publishing, Inc.). But before you run back to the bookstore or log on to your favorite book-selling Web site, go to one of these Web sites and install one of these fine products:

- ✔ **Norton AntiVirus** (www.symantec.com/nav)
- ✔ **McAfee VirusScan** (www.mcafee.com)
- ✔ **Grisoft AVG** (www.grisoft.com)
- ✔ **F-Prot** (www.fprot.org)

You can usually buy the software right there online and download it immediately, in addition to having a CD mailed to you. You can also get free trial versions that can help you cope with an urgent infection, in the event of an emergency.

Make sure to subscribe to the continuing-update services. The antivirus companies aren't just trying to wheedle more money out of you. (That's just a fringe benefit!) Really, though, new viruses appear all the time, and your virus checker needs to know about them in order to spot them. Last year's un-updated antivirus software is almost as bad as no antivirus software.

A few spam-filtering programs have built-in virus checkers. If you use a stand-alone spam filter, check to see whether it also scans for viruses.

Checking for Spyware and Adware

You can't always tell when you're downloading and installing software. Sometimes, programs sneak in when you click a link or button, or they arrive bundled with another program. These sneaky programs may contain viruses, may use your computer for their own purposes, and may report back to Mission Control with information about what you're doing. At other times, they may just pop up an advertisement while you're trying to surf around Web sites.

Programs that report back to their makers to tattle on the things you do and the places you go are *spyware*. Programs that contain advertising pop-ups or other advertisement-display mechanisms are *adware*.

Not all spyware is malicious. For example, Windows Media Player checks in with its home base whenever you click the Media Guide button or ask for information about an album. Other spyware may have more nefarious goals, such as telling the mother ship whenever you're shopping for a home mortgage.

Adware is often bundled in with some other piece of software that you're interested in using. Many music-stealing programs, like KaZaA and BearShare, have adware features that are responsible for many of the pop-up advertisements you see. So, if your kids are engaged in the federal crime of copyright theft and have installed software for doing it, that software may also be responsible for those annoying pop-up ads you're seeing.

Adware and spyware also have a darker side. Some adware companies also pay Web sites to surreptitiously install their adware whenever you visit that site. Still other adware gets installed while you're getting a "free gift" downloaded by a Web site. The gift may be a speed accelerator for your dial-up connection or some handy-dandy calendar or clock-synchronizing program. Unless you and your lawyer read the fine print (assuming that you can even find it), those free gifts are much like the famous Trojan horse — it looks fun but is really full of bad news!

Here are a few programs that can scan your computer for adware and spyware and remove what they find:

- ✔ **Ad-aware** (www.lavasoft.de/software/adaware)

- ✔ **Spybot Search and Destroy** (spybot.eon.net.au)

- ✔ **SpywareGuard** (www.wilderssecurity.net/spywareguard.html)

- ✔ **Webroot Spy Sweeper** (www.webroot.com/wb/products/spysweeper)

To learn more about how spyware and adware work and how to beat the privacy invaders at their own game, read *Internet Privacy For Dummies*, another fine yellow book by Wiley Publishing, Inc., written by two of your co-authors.

Don't Limit Yourself to One Web Page

The vast majority of Internet users use their Web browsers like this:

1. Open the browser to take up the entire screen.

2. Type an address or click a link.

3. Read stuff on the page.

4. Go back to Step 2.

If you want to go back to a page you were looking at a few minutes ago, you use the Back button or History list. And, while you're waiting for one page to load, you have nothing else to look at.

Why display only one Web page at a time? Almost all browsers can display lots of Web pages, each in a separate window. Some browsers can display multiple pages in one window, using either tabs or subwindows.

To open additional windows in your browser, press Ctrl+N or choose File➪New➪Window (this command works in almost all browsers). To switch from window to window, click in it.

Each window acts like a separate browser. Another way to open a new window is to right-click a link and choose Open in New Window from the menu that appears.

For example, if you're searching for information on the Web, you can use Google or another search engine to find a list of possibly useful sites. You can keep this list on-screen and open each site in a separate window.

Netscape 7 and Mozilla (our favorite browsers) can display lots of Web pages in one window by showing them on separate tabs. Press Ctrl+T to open a new tab in your browser window. You can open a bunch of tabs, as shown in Figure 15-4. To close a tab, click the X button to the right of the tabs. To switch from tab to tab, select a tab. The Opera tabs work about the same, except that you press Ctrl+Alt+N to open a new tab.

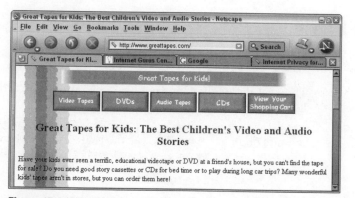

Figure 15-4: With Netscape and Mozilla, you can have lots of Web pages open, one on each tab.

Covering Your Tracks

Almost nobody who uses the Web is proud of each and every Web page they have visited. In fact, some people want to hide where they have been and are alarmed when they find out that Web browsers maintain a history of the pages they have viewed. The history feature wasn't added to track your every move, however. The idea was to make it easy for you to get back to pages you want to look at again.

If you want to erase your browser's history file, you can follow
these guidelines:

✔ **Internet Explorer:** Choose Tools➪Internet Options. On
the General tab, click the Clear History button.

✔ **Netscape 7 and Mozilla:** Choose Edit➪Preferences,
double-click the Navigator category if it's not open, and
click the History subcategory. Click the Clear History and
Clear Location Bar buttons.

✔ **Opera:** Choose File➪Delete Private Data, make sure that
the check boxes in the History section are cleared, and
click OK. (Clear the rest of the check boxes before clicking OK, unless you want a bunch of other information
deleted, too.)

There — that was easy! We aren't about to ask what sites you
have been looking at!

Finding Pages That Used to Be There

Rats! A friend e-mails you the address of a Web site that
sounds cool, but when you try the address, your browser displays a page that says Not Found or 404 Not Found or some
other cheery error message. What gives?

Web pages come and go — nothing about them is permanent.
A page that used to be there may have vanished. But more
likely, your (or your friend) spelled the address wrong. Here
are some things to try:

✔ **Shorten the address:** Try chopping things off the end of
the address. Web addresses (also known as URLs, or
Uniform Resource Locators), are in the form http://
hostname/pathname, where *hostname* is the name of the
computer on which the Web page is stored and *pathname*
is the exact location of the file. (You don't have to type
http://, by the way.) The pathname can be a series of
directory or folder names separated by slashes (/), followed by a filename. If the filename or the whole pathname is missing, the Web server displays a default page.

If you are getting an error message, leave off the filename (if any) of the last directory (folder) on the page. For example, if this line doesn't work (we guarantee that it doesn't):

```
http://net.gurus.com/windows/funfacts.html
```

try this one (still no good):

```
http://net.gurus.com/windows
```

and then this one (which works):

```
http://net.gurus.com
```

✔ **Google cache:** Perhaps the page used to exist, but has been moved or deleted. The Google Web site maintains a *cache* (temporary storage) of every site it indexes, so Google may still have a copy of the page. Search Google for text that you're sure appears on the page you want and then click the <u>Cached</u> link at the end of the entry for the site.

✔ **Wayback Machine:** The Wayback Machine, at www.archive.org/web/web.php, is an archive of Web pages. The page you're looking for may be stored there; it has copies of all kinds of Web sites over time. In the top box, type the Web address of the page you want and click the Take Me Back button. If the Wayback Machine archives the site, you see a list of dates on which the site was saved.

Has This Page Changed?

If a Web page arrives looking as though it has been through a blender, click the Refresh or Reload button on your browser's toolbar or press Ctrl+R. Ditto if you think that the page may have changed since it was loaded (for example, when you're looking at a page with up-to-the-minute news or scores).

Sending Mail to All Your Buddies

We *don't* want to encourage you to send spam! However, sometimes you need to send a message to a bunch of people, like all the people on a church committee or all members of your farflung extended family. People don't like getting messages with a hundred e-mail addresses at the top, for two reasons:

- You have to scroll down to see the message.

- You may not want all those other people to see your address.

Here's the right way to send a message to a bunch of people (more than ten or so, or any group of people who don't know each other): Type their addresses on the Bcc line, rather than on the To line, of the message. *Bcc,* which stands for *b*lind carbon *c*opy, harkens back to the days when people used carbon paper to make copies of letters. A *blind* copy is one that the rest of the recipients don't know about.

Not all e-mail programs have obvious Bcc lines when you're creating a message, but most have the feature hidden somewhere:

- **Outlook Express and Outlook** don't display a Bcc line (only To and Cc) in the New Message window. Choose View⇨All Headers (in Outlook Express) or View⇨Bcc Field (in Outlook if you don't use Word to compose messages) to display it. Or, click the To button (to the left of the To box) to see the Select Names or Recipients dialog box, where you can choose people to add to the Bcc line.

- **Netscape and Mozilla Mail** start with To in the address section of a new message, but you can click To and change it to Bcc.

- **Eudora, AOL Communicator, Hotmail, and MSN** display a Bcc line without your needing to do a thing!

- **AOL** doesn't display a Bcc box in the Write Mail window. Click the Address Book button, select someone from your address book, click the Send To button, and choose Bcc from the menu that appears.

> ✔ **Pegasus** displays the Bcc box on the Special tab when you're composing a message; select the tab or press F9.

Rather than leave the To line blank in your message, address it to yourself. Spam filters tend to throw away messages with no To address.

Index

FOR DUMMIES®

Helping you expand your horizons and realize your potential

PERSONAL FINANCE & BUSINESS

Investing
0-7645-2431-3

Home Buying
0-7645-5331-3

Grant Writing
0-7645-5307-0

Also available:

Accounting For Dummies
(0-7645-5314-3)

Business Plans Kit For Dummies
(0-7645-5365-8)

Managing For Dummies
(1-5688-4858-7)

Mutual Funds For Dummies
(0-7645-5329-1)

QuickBooks All-in-One Desk Reference For Dummies
(0-7645-1963-8)

Resumes For Dummies
(0-7645-5471-9)

Small Business Kit For Dummies
(0-7645-5093-4)

Starting an eBay Business For Dummies
(0-7645-1547-0)

Taxes For Dummies 2003
(0-7645-5475-1)

HOME, GARDEN, FOOD & WINE

Feng Shui
0-7645-5295-3

Gardening
0-7645-5130-2

Cooking
0-7645-5250-3

Also available:

Bartending For Dummies
(0-7645-5051-9)

Christmas Cooking For Dummies
(0-7645-5407-7)

Cookies For Dummies
(0-7645-5390-9)

Diabetes Cookbook For Dummies
(0-7645-5230-9)

Grilling For Dummies
(0-7645-5076-4)

Home Maintenance For Dummies
(0-7645-5215-5)

Slow Cookers For Dummies
(0-7645-5240-6)

Wine For Dummies
(0-7645-5114-0)

FITNESS, SPORTS, HOBBIES & PETS

Fitness
0-7645-5167-1

Golf
0-7645-5146-9

Guitar
0-7645-5106-X

Also available:

Cats For Dummies
(0-7645-5275-9)

Chess For Dummies
(0-7645-5003-9)

Dog Training For Dummies
(0-7645-5286-4)

Labrador Retrievers For Dummies
(0-7645-5281-3)

Martial Arts For Dummies
(0-7645-5358-5)

Piano For Dummies
(0-7645-5105-1)

Pilates For Dummies
(0-7645-5397-6)

Power Yoga For Dummies
(0-7645-5342-9)

Puppies For Dummies
(0-7645-5255-4)

Quilting For Dummies
(0-7645-5118-3)

Rock Guitar For Dummies
(0-7645-5356-9)

Weight Training For Dummies
(0-7645-5168-X)

Available wherever books are sold.
Go to www.dummies.com or call 1-877-762-2974 to order direct

FOR DUMMIES

A world of resources to help you grow

TRAVEL

0-7645-5453-0

0-7645-5438-7

0-7645-5444-1

Also available:

America's National Parks
For Dummies
(0-7645-6204-5)

Caribbean For Dummies
(0-7645-5445-X)

Cruise Vacations For
Dummies 2003
(0-7645-5459-X)

Europe For Dummies
(0-7645-5456-5)

Ireland For Dummies
(0-7645-6199-5)

France For Dummies
(0-7645-6292-4)

Las Vegas For Dummies
(0-7645-5448-4)

London For Dummies
(0-7645-5416-6)

Mexico's Beach Resorts
For Dummies
(0-7645-6262-2)

Paris For Dummies
(0-7645-5494-8)

RV Vacations For
Dummies
(0-7645-5443-3)

EDUCATION & TEST PREPARATION

0-7645-5194-9

0-7645-5325-9

0-7645-5249-X

Also available:

The ACT For Dummies
(0-7645-5210-4)

Chemistry For Dummies
(0-7645-5430-1)

English Grammar For
Dummies
(0-7645-5322-4)

French For Dummies
(0-7645-5193-0)

GMAT For Dummies
(0-7645-5251-1)

Inglés Para Dummies
(0-7645-5427-1)

Italian For Dummies
(0-7645-5196-5)

Research Papers For
Dummies
(0-7645-5426-3)

SAT I For Dummies
(0-7645-5472-7)

U.S. History For Dummies
(0-7645-5249-X)

World History For
Dummies
(0-7645-5242-2)

HEALTH, SELF-HELP & SPIRITUALITY

0-7645-5154-X

0-7645-5302-X

0-7645-5418-2

Also available:

The Bible For Dummies
(0-7645-5296-1)

Controlling Cholesterol
For Dummies
(0-7645-5440-9)

Dating For Dummies
(0-7645-5072-1)

Dieting For Dummies
(0-7645-5126-4)

High Blood Pressure For
Dummies
(0-7645-5424-7)

Judaism For Dummies
(0-7645-5299-6)

Menopause For Dummies
(0-7645-5458-1)

Nutrition For Dummies
(0-7645-5180-9)

Potty Training For
Dummies
(0-7645-5417-4)

Pregnancy For Dummies
(0-7645-5074-8)

Rekindling Romance For
Dummies
(0-7645-5303-8)

Religion For Dummies
(0-7645-5264-3)

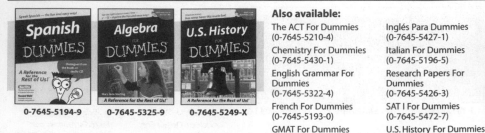

Available wherever books are sold. Go to www.dummies.com or call 1-877-762-2974 to order direct

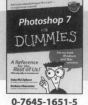